Every Day
~ Is A ~
Blessing

2003

Robin -

I'm so glad that we are
friends. Remember to be
good to yourself - you
deserve it ☺

Happy Birthday — Cynthia

EVERY DAY IS A BLESSING

365 Illuminations to Lift the Spirit

Rev. Aaron Zerah

WARNER BOOKS

An AOL Time Warner Company

Copyright © 2002 by Aaron Zerah
All rights reserved.

Warner Books, Inc., 1271 Avenue of the Americas, New York, NY 10020

Visit our Web site at www.twbookmark.com.

 An AOL Time Warner Company

Printed in the United States of America

First Printing: October 2002
10 9 8 7 6 5 4 3 2 1

Library of Congress Cataloging-in-Publication Data

Zerah, Aaron.
    Every day is a blessing: 365 illuminations to lift the spirit/Aaron Zerah.
       p. cm.
    ISBN 0-446-67898-8
       1. Meditations. 2. Devotional calendars. I. Title.

BL624.2 .Z46 2002
291.4'32—dc21   2002024047

Book design by Millicent Iacono
Cover design by Briaid Pearson
Cover photo by Richard H. Johnston/FPG

To my family and friends who make
every day a great day!

Acknowledgments

I feel blessed that today we have access to so many spiritual traditions from all over the world—and so many great people, too. I've had a marvelous time putting this book together, for by so doing I've deepened my connection to old friends and made many new ones. I am grateful for each and every source, and very happy to share their wisdom, wit, and wonder with you.

I especially want to thank my wife, Madhuri, for her love and personal sacrifice, and my young daughter, Sari, who loves my books and tells people, "My Abba writes."

I am also very grateful to Nancy Ellis, my dear friend and agent; Jackie Joiner and Molly Chehak, my delightful editors; and Coral O'Reilly and Donna Bain of Coast Copy Centre, whose goodwill and good humor miraculously transformed my handwritten manuscript into a lovely book.

And, dear reader, one more thanks—to you, for reading and enjoying *Every Day Is a Blessing*. I'd love to hear from you, so please . . . email zerah2@hotmail.com.

Many Blessings,
Rev. Aaron Zerah

A Personal Note from the Author

Dear One:

There's an old Russian proverb that says: every day is a messenger of God. That's what I hope *Every Day Is a Blessing* will be for you—a daily message that lifts your spirit and delights your soul.

When you look inside, you'll discover a vast array of wise sayings, proverbs, and stories from the world's great spiritual traditions and cultures. You'll also find hundreds of quotes, jokes, and anecdotes from many of the greatest souls of our planet. People like Jesus, Buddha, and Mother Teresa; the Dalai Lama, Muhammad, and Anne Frank; Emily Dickinson, St. Francis of Assisi, Billy Graham, Chief Seattle, and Confucius. And then there's Muhammad Ali, Leonardo da Vinci, Woody Allen, Albert Einstein, Duke Ellington, Eleanor Roosevelt, Pablo Picasso, and John F. Kennedy. In short, there's everybody from Aesop to (including my one entry) Zerah. For your information and enlightenment, I've put together a Roster of Great Souls at the back of the book that provides a brief description of each person.

Every Day Is a Blessing has a short reading for each special and holy day of the year—plus an extra one on February 29 for leap years. It is designed to be read at the breakfast table, on the bus or subway, at breaks for a boost on the job, or in bed to sweetly complete your day. Whenever and wherever works for you is just great.

I'm going to quote here one additional great soul—my four-year-old daughter, Sari. One morning she said, "Abba, I've got something to tell you." "Okay, Sari," I said, "what is it?" Sari paused thoughtfully and then said, "Today is . . . today!"

In Love and Kindness,
Rev. Aaron Zerah

EVERY DAY
IS A
BLESSING

The man who removed the mountain began
by carrying away small stones.

—*Chinese Proverb*

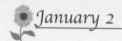

The moment one definitely commits oneself
then Providence moves too.

All sorts of things occur to help one
that would never otherwise have occurred.

A whole stream of events issues from the commitment,
raising in one's favor all manner
of unforeseen incidents and meetings
and material assistance
which no one could have dreamt
would come one's way.

Whatever you can do,
or dream you can, begin it.
Boldness has genius, power, and magic in it.
Begin it now.

—*Goethe*

If we don't change the direction we're going,
we're likely to end up where we're headed.

—*Chinese Proverb*

He who is outside the door has already a
good part of his journey behind him.

—*Dutch Proverb*

It is good to have an end to journey towards;
but it is the journey that matters in the end.

—*Ursula K. Le Guin*

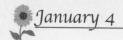

The winds of grace are always blowing,
but you have to raise the sail.

—*Ramakrishna*

When the saint Nam Dev was but a very young boy, his father entrusted him to make the daily milk offering to the divine. In his father's absence, Nam Dev was to place the milk before the statue in their home, and with great reverence the young boy did just as his father had instructed.

Nam Dev's father always drank the milk after the ritual offering, but the pure-hearted Nam Dev did not know this. When the statue did not take the milk he brought, Nam Dev pleaded, "My Lord, please drink the offering before you." But the statue did not drink. Nam Dev was persistent. "My Lord," he cried out, "do you wish to see a fight in our house? If you do not take this milk, my father will be very angry with me."

Nam Dev kept imploring the statue in this way until at last a hand stretched out—and the statue drank up all the milk.

—*Traditional Sikh Story*

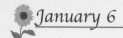

To see what is right and not to do it is want of courage.

—*Confucius*

Courage is fear that has said its prayers.

—*Karl Barth*

It is the chiefest point of happiness
that a man is willing to be what he is.

—*Desiderius Erasmus*

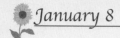

Have patience with all things
but first of all with yourself.

—*St. Francis de Sales*

The Lord is my pace-setter: I shall not rush.
He makes me stop and rest for quiet intervals.
He provides me with images of stillness
Which restore my serenity.
He leads me in the way of efficiency
Through calmness of mind
And His guidance is peace.
Even though I have a great many things
To accomplish each day,
I will not fret.

For His presence is here.
His timelessness,
His all-importance,
Will keep me in balance.
He prepares refreshment and renewal in the midst of activity
By anointing my mind with the oil of tranquillity.
My cup of joyous energy overflows.
Surely harmony and effectiveness shall be the fruit of my hours,
For I shall walk in the pace of my Lord
And dwell in His house forever.

—*Psalm 23 (Japanese Version)*

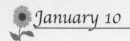

Do all the good you can
By all the means you can
In all the ways you can
In all the places you can
To all the people you can
As long as ever you can.

—*John Wesley*

When you arise in the morning,
give thanks for the morning light,
for your life and strength.
Give thanks for your food
and the joy of living.

—Chief Tecumseh

If the only prayer you say in your whole life is
"thank you," that would be enough.

—Meister Eckhart

Gratitude is heaven itself.

—William Blake

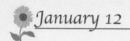

The one who takes things too seriously all day long has no joy in his life. The one who wastes the day in seeking amusement cannot maintain a position of fortune.

—*Ptah-hotep*

No one has a right to sit down and feel hopeless. There's too much work to do.

—*Dorothy Day*

One bitter cold winter morning, at the first light of dawn, the poor janitor came in to clean the synagogue. When he finished his work, he put down his broom and began to say his prayers. "Oh God," he whispered, "before you I am the smallest of the small. I am nothing."

Meanwhile the shammes, the rabbi's assistant, had come in and was saying his own prayers on the other side of the synagogue. "Oh Lord," the shammes said, "I am nothing but a simple shammes. Please hear my prayer." Then the rabbi joined him and prayed. "Almighty God, you know I am just the rabbi of a small congregation, nothing in your eyes, but listen to my prayer."

When the shammes and rabbi were done praying, they crept near to the janitor. When they heard the janitor's prayer, the shammes elbowed the rabbi in the ribs and said: "Look who thinks *he's* nothing!"

—*Traditional Jewish Joke*

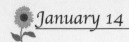

If people knew how hard I have to work to gain my
mastery, it would not seem wonderful at all.

—*Michelangelo*

All are caught in an inescapable network of mutuality,
tied in a single garment of destiny. Whatever affects one directly,
affects all indirectly. I can never be what I ought to be until you are
what you ought to be, and you can never be what you ought to
be until I am what I ought to be.

—*Martin Luther King Jr.*

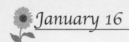

In the depths of winter, I finally learned that
within me there lay an invincible summer.

—*Albert Camus*

A great Mongol general had led his army in victory after victory. Most of Central Asia, except the grand city of Samarkand, was theirs. The general was confident they could conquer the city, despite the fact that his soldiers were war-weary and greatly outnumbered. He was sure of their destiny, but equally certain he could not force his soldiers to fight.

So the wise general gathered the troops around a sacred altar to pray for guidance from the gods. Then he took out, for all to see, a large gold coin with a face on one side. "If it shows the face when I toss it," the general declared, "it is a sign from the gods of our victory in Samarkand." The coin landed face-up and the soldiers, believing the gods were behind them, easily captured the city.

After the battle, one of the soldiers told the general: "When we know the gods are with us, there is nothing between us and our destiny." The general laughed and brought out the large gold coin. There was a face on both sides.

—*Classical Chinese Story*

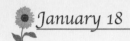

Habit is habit, and not to be kicked out the door at any
time, but coaxed down the stairs little by little.

—*Mark Twain*

May no one who ever meets me
Have a meeting of little consequence.
May the simple fact of our meeting
Assist in the fulfillment of their wishes.
May I be a lamp
In the darkness of life,
A home for the homeless,
And a servant to the world.

—*Ancient Buddhist Blessing*

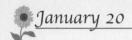

Leadership means not giving orders
to others, but giving of yourself.

—*East African Tribal Proverb*

Do not disregard evil, saying, "It will not come unto me." By the falling of drops, even a water jar is filled; likewise the fool, gathering little by little, fills himself with evil.

Do not disregard merit, saying, "It will not come unto me." By the falling of drops, even a water jar is filled; likewise the wise man, gathering little by little, fills himself with good.

*—from the Dhammapada
(Sacred Book of Buddhism)*

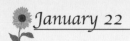
God dwells wherever man lets Him in.
                                        —*Martin Buber*

Wherever you live is your temple if you treat it like one.
                                        —*Buddha*

Wherever my travels may lead, paradise is where I am.
                                        —*Voltaire*

Home is the place where, when you have to go there,
they have to take you in.

—*Robert Frost*

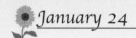

What a wonderful life I've had.
I only wish I had realized it sooner.

—*Colette*

He who offers to me with devotion
only a leaf, or a flower, or a fruit,
or even a little water,
this I accept with joy,
because with a pure heart
it was offered with Love.

—*from the Bhagavad Gita*
(Hindu Holy Book)

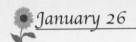

A person who hides the truth that
he is sick cannot expect to be cured.

—*Ethiopian Proverb*

The main reason for healing is love.

—*Paracelsus*

Chuang-tzu was fishing in the P'u River when two high officials sent by the prince of Ch'u came to ask him to take charge of the administration of the state. Chuang-tzu went on fishing and without turning his head said, "I have heard that in Ch'u there is a sacred tortoise which has been dead now some three thousand years. And that the prince keeps his tortoise carefully enclosed in a chest on the altar of his ancestral people. Now would this tortoise rather be dead and have its remains revered, or be alive and wagging its tail in the mud?" The two officials answered: "It would rather be alive." "Then begone!" cried Chuang-tzu. "I too will wag my tail in the mud."

—*from the Book of Chuang-tzu*
(Classical Taoist Text)

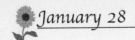

Never be ashamed to own you have been in the wrong;
'tis but saying you are wiser today than you were yesterday.

—*Jonathan Swift*

To be really sorry for one's errors is like
opening the door of Heaven.

—*Hazrat Inayat Khan*

A hungry wolf came out of the woods and into the little town of Gubbio. In the night he howled and the next morning the inhabitants discovered that a fellow villager had fallen victim to the wolf. Day after day, upon awakening, the people of Gubbio found another neighbor dead and mangled in the streets.

Deeply afraid, they decided to seek the help of St. Francis, the holy man who everyone said spoke with all of God's creatures. They wanted St. Francis to tell the wolf to obey the commandments and stop murdering his neighbors. If the wolf did not listen, then the holy man was to instruct the beast to live somewhere else—anywhere but Gubbio.

And so St. Francis went to the forest to speak to Brother Wolf about the fears of the townsfolk. When he returned, everyone was anxious to hear his report. "Good people of Gubbio," St. Francis said, "there is an answer for your predicament. You must simply find a way to feed this wolf of yours."

—Traditional Italian Story

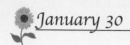

The poor Mullah Nasreddin was reduced to living on a diet of chickpeas and bread, while his neighbor dined on fancy delicacies provided by the King himself.

One day his neighbor said to Nasreddin: "If you were truly wise you would learn to flatter the King and obey his every whim like I do. Then you would not have to live on chickpeas and bread." Nasreddin answered, "And if you would learn to live on chickpeas and bread like I do, then you would not have to flatter the King and obey his every whim."

—*Traditional Sufi Story*

The force of arms cannot do what peace does.
If you can gain your desired end with sugar, why use poison?

—*from the Somadeva*
(Jain Sacred Text)

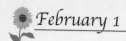

You cannot prevent the birds of sorrow from
flying over your head, but you can prevent them
from building nests in your hair.

—*Chinese Proverb*

I find letters from God dropped in the street,
and every one is signed by God's name.

—*Walt Whitman*

There is no way of telling people that they are
all walking around shining like the sun.

—*Thomas Merton*

People see God every day; they just don't recognize him.

—*Pearl Bailey*

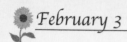

We are not human beings having a spiritual experience.
We are spiritual beings having a human experience.

—*Pierre Teilhard de Chardin*

In the hills of Japan a long while ago, two cats lived together. One was black and very big and the other a tabby, much smaller in size. They were the best of friends, these two, and were very good to each other.

One day, each of them found a most delightful treat—a fresh, sweet rice cake. The cats shouted, "They smell more wonderful than a fat field mouse!"

Then the two cats sat down together to look at each other's cakes and compare them. They soon noticed that the big cat had a small cake and the small cat a much bigger one.

"I'm big, so I should have the big cake," the black cat complained. "Let us swap." But the little tabby hissed and threatened to bite his friend. "I am small, so I need to eat the bigger one. I will never trade with you."

They started calling each other names, and soon they were snarling and trying to scratch each other. For hours the big cat and the small cat chased each other around the trees and howled.

Finally, the black cat, out of breath, said, "Let us stop this fighting and go see the wise monkey, and let him make equal shares of the rice cakes for us."

As the cakes were already beginning to get hard and stale, the small cat agreed. So they hurried into the forest, calling out, "Mr. Monkey! Mr. Monkey!" At last there he was, sitting in a high branch of a tree, wearing a red hat, and holding a set of golden scales in his hands that he used to solve problems just like the one the two cats had.

After listening to the excited cats, the wise monkey soon said with a serious voice, "How right you were to come to me."

He promised that each cat would get an equal share, and with that he took the two cakes from them and put one on each side of the scale. "Your quarrel was quite understandable," the wise monkey said. "The big piece is much heavier. I will have to take a bite to even them out." And he did.

But he took too much, and now the other cake was the heavier one. "Oh no," the wise monkey said. "Now I shall have to take a bite out of the other one." So he did, but once again, the two cakes were not equal. The wise monkey kept taking bites out of one and then the other, and both cakes got smaller and smaller. The two cats cried out, "That's enough!" and "They must be even now!" but the clever monkey paid no attention to them. He kept weighing and eating and weighing and eating until he had eaten up all of the rice cakes.

"Well," he said to the cats, "you see, the cakes are equal now. That is what you came for, is it not? Now there is nothing left for you to quarrel about."

And the two cats never did quarrel again.

—*Traditional Japanese Story*

There is no expedient to which a man will not
go to avoid the real labor of thinking.

—*Thomas Edison*

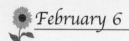

Any disaster you can survive is an improvement
in your character, your stature, and your life.

—*Joseph Campbell*

When we accept what happens to us and make
the best of it, we are praising God.

—*St. Teresa of Avila*

The best and most beautiful things in the world cannot be
seen or even touched. They must be felt in the heart.

—Helen Keller

Happy are the pure in heart for they shall see God.

—Jesus

Words that come from the heart enter the heart.

—Abraham ibn Ezra

There is a polish for everything that becomes rusty,
and the polish for the heart is the remembrance of God.

—Muhammad

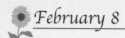

The Holy Spirit is our harpist and all strings
which are touched in love must sound.

—*Mechtild of Magdeburg*

The Creator, Fidi Mukullu, made everything in the world. He made the animals and people and food for them to eat.

He planted banana trees in the earth, too. When the bananas became ripe, he sent the sun to gather them. The sun brought a full basket back and Fidi Mukullu asked, "Did you eat any of the bananas?" The sun said that he did not, but Fidi Mukullu decided to test him. He put the sun in a deep hole and asked, "When do you want to get out?" "Early tomorrow morning," said the sun. "If you told me the truth, you will arise then," said Fidi Mukullu, and the sun did arise just so the next morning. The moon, too, was tested, and having told the truth like the sun, came out of the pit to find her place in the sky.

Then came man's turn. He gathered the bananas, but ate some on the way to Fidi Mukullu. When questioned, he said he had eaten none. The man wished to come out of the deep hole in the earth in five days, but once into the earth he never came out. Fidi Mukullu said, "The sun appears again, the moon appears again, but man, because he did not tell the truth, dies and does not appear again."

—Traditional Central African Story

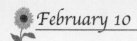

Every man's life is a fairy tale,
written by God's fingers.

—*Hans Christian Andersen*

A man who wished to live a saintly life went to his teacher and said, "O guru, bringer of light into the darkness, how shall I become a saint, a true sadhu? Please tell me."

The guru told the man to own as little as possible and to live as simply as he could. So the student gave up his possessions and moved to a tiny shack far from other people. Every day, after his morning devotional rituals, he'd wash and hang out to dry his loincloth, the only thing he owned. One day he discovered birds had pecked holes in it, and since he had nothing else to wear, he went to the village to beg for a new one.

A few days later the new loincloth met an identical fate. "Well," the villagers said, "you not only need a loincloth, but you need a cat to protect it from the birds." So the man asked for and got a cat.

Then he needed to beg for milk to feed the cat. After a time the villagers grew weary of giving him milk for the cat. "You need to keep a cow," they told the poor man.

So he went and asked for a cow. Once he had the cow, he needed hay to feed the cow. His neighbors told him to stop begging and to grow his own hay, that there was plenty of farmland to be had.

So the simple man became a farmer. Soon he had to build barns and hire laborers. And then, because he was a landholder, he married, had children, and spent his days like all the other busy householders.

After a while, his guru came to visit the area and the prosperous farm. Finding the farm filled with goods and buzzing with servants, the guru inquired of one, "A poor holy man used to dwell in these parts. Do you know where he has gone?" Receiving no answer, the guru went to the main house, where he ran into his surprised student. "What happened?" the guru asked.

The man fell at the feet of his master and said pitifully, "My Lord, it all started with a single loincloth."

—Traditional Hindu Story

Determine that the thing can and shall
be done and then find the way.

—*Abraham Lincoln*

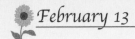

Love does not consist in gazing at each other,
but in looking outward together in the same direction.

—*Antoine de Saint Exupéry*

When two people are at one
in their innermost hearts
They shatter even the strength of
iron or of bronze.

And when two people understand
each other in their innermost hearts
Their words are sweet and strong
like the fragrance of orchids.

—*from the I Ching*
(Ancient Chinese Sacred Text)

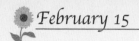

What lies behind us and what lies before us
are tiny matters compared to what lies within us.

—*Ralph Waldo Emerson*

The crisis of yesterday is the joke of tomorrow.

—*H. G. Wells*

Holiness consists in doing the
will of God with a smile.

—*Mother Teresa*

For twenty years, an old woman took care of a monk so that he could meditate and seek enlightenment. He lived in a little hut the old woman had built for him, and there his food was brought.

One day, the old woman decided to check on the progress of the monk and sent a young woman, experienced in providing bodily pleasure, to visit him. The young woman caressed the monk in seductive ways and invitingly asked, "Now what is your desire?" The monk responded, "There is nothing warm here. Just an old tree growing on cold wintry stones."

Hearing the story, the old woman became very angry. She shouted, "I kept that fake alive for twenty years and he shows you not a bit of kindness! It wasn't necessary for him to have been passionate, just a little compassion would have been enough!"

And that was the last time the old woman fed the monk.

—Traditional Zen Buddhist Story

If your parents take care of you up to the time
you cut your teeth, you take care of them
when they lose theirs.

—West African Proverb

Let me show you the straight path to God:
Work hard at honest labor with your own hands to support yourself,
always remember God, and share the fruits of your labors.

If people retreat to the mountains to recite the name of God,
who will put out the fire of the burning world?
—*Guru Nanak*

When people say to you "it's good to cry,"
they don't mean you ought to cry all the time.
When they say to you "stop your crying,"
they don't mean you should always act like a clown.

—*Shah Naqshband*

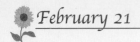

Patience serves as protection against wrongs as clothes
do against cold. For if you put on more clothes as the cold
increases, it will have no power to hurt you. So in like manner
you must grow in patience when you meet with great wrongs
and they will be powerless to vex your mind.

—*Leonardo da Vinci*

Labor to keep alive in your breast that spark
of celestial fire called conscience.

—*George Washington*

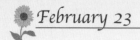

My favorite piece of music is the one
we hear all the time if we are quiet.

—*John Cage*

If I am not for myself, who then will be for me?
If I am only for myself, who am I? And if not now, when?

—Rabbi Hillel

At fifteen, I set my heart upon learning. At thirty, I had planted my feet upon firm ground. At forty, I no longer suffered from perplexities. At fifty, I knew what were the biddings of Heaven. At sixty, I heard them with a docile ear. At seventy, I could follow the dictates of my own heart, for what I desired no longer overstepped the boundaries of right.

—*Confucius*

They deem me mad because I will not sell my days for gold;
and I deem them mad because they think my days have a price.

—*Kahlil Gibran*

A keen sense of humor helps us to overlook the unbecoming,
understand the unconventional, tolerate the unpleasant,
and outlast the unbearable.

—*Billy Graham*

Out of work as usual, Mullah Nasreddin awoke one day and informed his wife, "I no longer will be seeking employment. I work now only for Allah." Not one to be put off easily, she replied, "If that is true, please ask Allah for your back wages." "A good idea," thought Nasreddin, and he proceeded to his backyard and prayed for a hundred pieces of gold as his just reward. Overhearing him, his well-to-do neighbor decided to play a joke on the simple mullah. He hurriedly put a hundred gold pieces in a sack and, without being seen, threw the sack over the fence at Nasreddin's feet.

The mullah took the gold, and he and his wife began to spend it. Enough was enough, and the neighbor soon demanded his money back. Nasreddin refused, claiming that the money was a gift of providence. The neighbor became irate and threatened to bring Nasreddin before a judge. After a moment's thought, Nasreddin said, "Let's go right now. But so the court will not be prejudiced against me, lend me a fine robe and a horse so we can appear on an equal footing." The neighbor agreed, and off they went. At the court the neighbor stated his complaint. Then it was Nasreddin's turn. His defense was insanity; Nasreddin claimed that his neighbor was insane! "What is your evidence for this?" the judge inquired. "If you ask the man, he'll say that not only was the money his, but the fine horse I rode here, and this very robe I'm wearing, too," Nasreddin said calmly. "But that is indeed so," cried the exasperated neighbor. "Case dismissed," said the judge.

—*Traditional Sufi Story*

Living is a form of not being sure, not knowing
what next or how. The moment you know how, you begin
to die a little. The artist never entirely knows. We guess.
We may be wrong, but we take leap after leap in the dark.

—*Agnes de Mille*

There are two ways to live your life.
One is as though nothing is a miracle.
The other is as though everything is a miracle.

—*Albert Einstein*

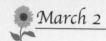

A man's own mind sometimes has a way of telling him
more than seven watchmen posted on a high tower.

—*from Wisdom of Ben Sira*
(Sacred Book of Judaism)

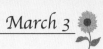
Keep a green tree alive in your heart and a
songbird may come to sing there.

—*Chinese Proverb*

In the marketplace, Rabbi Beroka often met the prophet Elijah, who descended from heaven to help the poor and the pious. One day Rabbi Beroka asked Elijah, "Does any soul in this market have a place in the world to come?" As they were talking, two men came by and Elijah said, "Those two have a place in the world to come."

Rabbi Beroka walked up to them and asked, "What do you do?" They answered, "We are jesters. When we see people sad or depressed, we try to cheer them up, and when we see two people arguing, we work hard to make peace between them."

—*from the Babylonian Talmud*
(Sacred Book of Judaism)

O Thou, who kindly doth provide
For ev'ry creature's want!
We bless the God of Nature wide
For all Thy goodness lent.
And if it please Thee, heavenly Guide,
May never worse be sent;
But, whether granted or denied,
Lord, bless us with content.

—*Robert Burns*

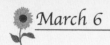

Once the Roman emperor Hadrian was walking along the road near Tiberias in Galilee, and he saw an old man planting fig trees.

"If you had worked in your early years, old man," he said, "you would not have to work now so late in your life."

"I have worked both early and late," the man said, "and what pleased the Lord He has done with me."

"How old are you?" asked Hadrian.

"A hundred years old," the man said.

"A hundred years old, and you are still digging up the earth to plant trees!" said Hadrian. "Do you truly expect to eat the fruit of those trees?"

"If I am worthy, I will eat," answered the old man. "But if not, as my father worked for me, so I am working for my children."

—*Traditional Jewish Story*

When eating a fruit, think of the person who planted the tree.

—*Vietnamese Proverb*

It is better to be
In God's hands and be poor
Than to have your wealth
In your own storehouse.

It is better to have
Bread with a happy heart
Than great riches
And a troubled heart.

—Amenemope

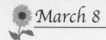

If you want others to be happy, practice compassion.
If you want to be happy, practice compassion.

—*Dalai Lama*

The beating heart of the universe is holy joy.
—*Martin Buber*

You will go out in joy
and be led forth in peace;
the mountains and hills before you
will burst into song.

—*from the Book of Isaiah*
(Hebrew Scriptures)

Keep knocking and the joy inside will eventually
open a window and look out to see who is there.
—*Rumi*

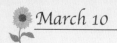

The seed of God is in us. Given an intelligent and
hardworking farmer, it will thrive and grow up to God,
whose seed it is; and accordingly its fruit will be God-nature.
Pear seeds grow into pear trees, nut seeds into nut trees,
and God seeds into God.

—*Meister Eckhart*

He that looks at the wind does not sow his seeds. And he that observes the clouds shall not reap a harvest. As you know not the way of the wind, nor how the bones grow inside a child in the mother's womb, even so you know not the works of God who makes all things.

In the morning, then, you sow your seeds and in the evening do not withhold your hand. For you do not know which shall prosper, this or that, or whether both shall prove to be equally good.

—from the Book of Ecclesiastes
(Hebrew Scriptures)

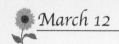

It is not a matter of thinking a great deal but of loving a great deal, so do whatever arouses you most to love.

—*St. Teresa of Avila*

Don't ask yourself what the world needs.
Ask yourself what makes you come alive,
and go do that, because what the world needs
is people who have come alive.

—*Howard Thurman*

How wonderful it is that nobody need wait a single moment before starting to improve the world.

—*Anne Frank*

A deer came to a pool to drink, and stopped to look at his image in the water. When he saw his mighty antlers, the deer swelled with pride. When he saw his legs reflected in the water, the deer was sorry that they appeared to be so skinny and weak.

While he was thinking these thoughts, a lion suddenly ran right at him. The deer took off and quickly outran the lion, for a deer's strength is in his legs and a lion's strength is in the heart. So as long as the deer kept running on the plain, he kept ahead of the lion.

But when the deer ran into the forest, his antlers got stuck on some tree branches and the lion caught up to him. Just as the lion was about to kill him, the deer sadly said to himself, "How strange things are! My scrawny legs almost got me away to safety, and my magnificent antlers have cost me my life!"

—*Fable of Aesop*

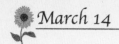

A student asked his teacher, Fenglin: "Master, do you enjoy sex and money?" Fenglin replied, "Yes, indeed." The student was greatly surprised. "But you are a spiritual teacher," the student sputtered. "How can you enjoy sex and money?" Fenglin answered, "So few are truly grateful."

—*Traditional Zen Buddhist Story*

You are not yet blessed, if the multitude
does not laugh at you.

—*Seneca*

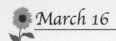

If you dream it, you can do it.

—*Walt Disney*

May the road rise to meet you,
May the wind be always at your back,
May the sun shine warm upon your face,
The rains fall soft upon your fields,
And until we meet again, may
God hold you in the hollow of his hand.

—Traditional Irish Blessing

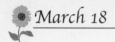

One who praises you for qualities you lack will
next be found blaming you for faults not yours.

—*Ali*

A great man calls attention to the good points
in others; he does not call attention to their defects.
A small man does just the opposite.

—*Confucius*

Each man takes care that his neighbor shall
not cheat him. But a day comes when he begins
to care that he does not cheat his neighbor.
Then all goes well—he has changed his
market-cart into a chariot of the sun.

—*Ralph Waldo Emerson*

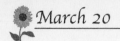

When I walk through thy woods,
may my right foot and my left foot
be harmless to the little creatures
that move in its grasses: as it is said
by the mouth of thy prophet,
They shall not hurt nor destroy
in all my holy mountain.

—*Rabbi Moshe Hakotun*

There is a crack in everything.
That's how the light gets in.

—Leonard Cohen

You must be lamps unto yourselves.

—Buddha

What is to give light must burn.

—Viktor Frankl

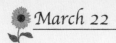

Walk on a rainbow trail, walk on a trail of song,
and all about you will be beauty.
There is a way out of every dark mist,
over a rainbow trail.

—*Traditional Dineh/Navajo Tribal Song*
(Native American)

The humble Rabbi Zusya of Hanipol was very old and nearing death. Thinking of the world to come, he said, "If they ask me 'Why were you not more like Abraham?' I will have an easy answer; I was not born with a great intellect like Abraham. If they ask me 'Why were you not more like Moses?' I will also have an easy answer; I was not born with his gift for leadership. But if they ask me 'Why were you not more like Zusya?' I will have no answer to give."

—*Traditional Chassidic Jewish Story*

The things, good Lord, that we pray for,
give us the grace to labor for.

—*Thomas More*

God give me work
Till my life shall end
And life
Till my work is done.

—*Epitaph on an Old*

English Tombstone

Blessed is he who has found his work.
Let him ask no other blessedness.

—*Thomas Carlyle*

There are halls in the heavens above
that open but to the voice of song.

> —*from the Zohar*
> *(Ancient Mystical Text of Judaism)*

We can make our minds so like still water that beings
gather about us, that they may see their own images, and
so live for a moment with a clearer, perhaps even
with a fiercer life because of our quiet.

—*William Butler Yeats*

It is not necessary to have great things to do.
I turn my little omelet in the pan for the love of God.

—*Brother Lawrence*

Reb Lieb was leaving his village to begin his studies of the holy books, the Torah, with the learned rabbi Dov Baer. A friend asked, "What are you going to learn from such a great teacher, the Maggid of Meseritz?"

"I am not going to gain knowledge of holy scripture from him," Reb Lieb said. "I am going to watch how he ties his shoes."

—Traditional Chassidic
Jewish Story

Do not fear mistakes. There are none.

—*Miles Davis*

Our deepest fear is not that we are inadequate.
Our deepest fear is that we are powerful beyond measure.

—*Marianne Williamson*

The main thing in life is not to be afraid of being human.

—*Pablo Casals*

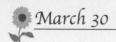

Do not open your mouth
But keep guard over your lips
When you are provoked and angered.

If you speak out in haste
You shall have to atone later
So soothe your soul with silence.

—*from Ancient Sumerian Tablets*

A man wanted to have a lion tattooed on his back, but as soon as the tattoo artist pricked him with the first needle he cried out, "You're killing me! Which part of the lion are you doing?" "I'm doing the tail first," said the tattoo artist. "Leave off the tail then," shouted the man. So the tattoo artist began again, and the man screamed again in pain. "Which part are you doing now?" "The ear," said the artist. "Leave off the ear," demanded the man. So he started once more and the man shrieked, "What part of the lion is that?" "The belly of the lion," answered the tattooist. "I want a lion with no belly," ordered the man. The frustrated tattooist had had enough. He threw down his needles and said, "A lion that has no tail, no ear, and no belly? Who can make a creature like that? Even God did not!"

—*Rumi*

One day the Emperor Akbar complained to his counselor, Birbal, "I am allowed to meet only wise and learned men. Bring me the ten greatest fools in the kingdom." So Birbal brought him a collection of fools. The first man, riding a horse, carried a bundle of firewood on his head, reasoning that the burden would be too heavy for the horse if he placed it on the saddle. Another was found looking at night for a ring he had lost, searching not where he dropped it in the dark under a tree, but in a nearby clearing where the light was better. Birbal brought eight such fools to the king, who soon reminded him that he had asked for ten. "There are ten," the trickster laughed, "including you and me, the two biggest fools of all—you for giving me such a ridiculous order, and me for obeying it!"

—*Traditional Hindu Story*

Only a fool tests the depth of the water with both feet.

—*African Proverb*

Therefore I tell you, do not be anxious about your life, what you shall eat or what you shall drink, nor about your body, what you shall put on. Is not life more than food, and the body more than clothing? Look at the birds of the air; they neither sow nor reap nor gather into barns, and yet your heavenly Father feeds them. Are you not much more than they?

—Jesus

The chakora bird longs for the moonlight,
The lotus longs for sunrise,
The bee longs to drink the flower's nectar,
Even so my heart anxiously longs for you, O Lord.

—*from the Basavanna
(Sacred Hindu Text)*

If a man hasn't discovered something that
he will die for, he isn't fit to live.

—*Martin Luther King Jr.*

When you are proclaiming peace with your lips,
be careful to have it even more fully in your heart.

—*St. Francis of Assisi*

If you have two pieces of silver,
sell one and buy a lily.

—*Greek Proverb*

Consider the trees which allow the birds to
perch and fly away without either inviting them to
stay or desiring them never to depart. If your heart
can be like this, you will be near to the way.

> —*Traditional Zen*
> *Buddhist Teaching*

The Dalai Lama of Tibet was a very young boy when he had his first gardening experience. He most carefully and assiduously planted his seeds in a well-prepared bed. Satisfied, he returned to his holy abode. The next day he came to see his plants and flowers growing, but there was nothing showing. He went home and came back the following day once more, expecting to see the new plants growing. There were none. On the third day, seeing that again nothing was there, in frustration the Dalai Lama dug out all the seeds he had placed in the garden.

Now, he laughs and says, "You plant; you water; it blossoms."

—*Story of the Dalai Lama*

Beware of all enterprises that require new clothes.
—*Henry David Thoreau*

Three things drain a person's health: worry, travel, and sin.
Three things restore a person's good spirits:
beautiful sounds, sights, and smells.

—*from the Babylonian Talmud*
(Sacred Book of Judaism)

Never underestimate the healing effects of beauty.

—*Florence Nightingale*

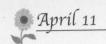

Whatever a man fears may happen to him is only a matter of probability—either it will happen or it will not happen. And just as it is possible that something painful, worrisome and fearful may happen, it is also possible that, because of his reliance on God, the reverse of what he feared may happen. Because, both what he feared and the reverse are possible.

—*Moses Maimonides*

If you keep on saying things are going to be bad, you have a good chance of being a prophet.

—*Isaac Bashevis Singer*

A bird sings like a flute
In a hidden grove of willows.
The golden-threaded trees sway gracefully.

The mountain valley hushes
As the clouds return.
A breeze carries the fragrance of apricot flowers.

Here I have sat the whole day,
Enveloped by peace,
Until my mind is cleansed inside and out.

Free of cares and idle thoughts,
I wish to tell you how I feel,
Yet, words are lacking.

If you come to this grove,
We can then compare our notes.

—*Fa-Yen*

Yours are the hands with which he is still to bless.
—*St. Teresa of Avila*

A poor farmer's prize horse disappeared one day, last seen heading for the country of the barbarians. The other farmers, poor like him, knew how much the horse meant to the family and expressed their sympathy. The old farmer said only, "How do you know this isn't good fortune?"

A few months passed. Lo and behold, the farmer's horse came back, bringing with it another horse, strong and of new stock. The neighbors congratulated the farmer for his good luck. The farmer was terse. "How do you know this doesn't forbode disaster?" The peasants merely shook their heads and went back to their work.

The two horses mated, and soon the family had many fine horses and became very rich. The farmer's son, with leisure time now on his hands, took a fancy to riding his beautiful horse, and one day he fell off and broke his hip. Once again came the other farmers to offer condolences and to wish the father a quick recovery for his son. He told them, "How do you know this is not a good thing?"

Well, the hip did not heal well and the son became lame as a result. Some time went by, and the barbarians crossed the frontier. War had begun, and all able-bodied young men were required to fight. Nine out of ten of them died. The young farmer, limp and all, stayed home and alive.

—*Traditional Taoist Story*

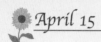

God, Give us grace to accept with serenity the
things that cannot be changed, courage to change
the things which should be changed, and the
wisdom to distinguish the one from the other.

—*Reinhold Niebuhr*

One going to take a pointed stick to poke a baby bird
should first try it on himself to feel how it hurts.

—*West African Proverb*

# April 17

If one person tells you that you have the ears of an ass,
pay no attention. If two should tell you,
go get yourself a saddle.

—*Hebrew Proverb*

Many waters cannot quench love;
Rivers cannot wash it away.
If one were to give
All the wealth of his house for love,
It would be utterly scorned.

—*from the Song of Songs*
(Hebrew Scriptures)

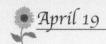

I believe in the sun even when it is not shining.
I believe in love even when feeling it not.
I believe in God even when he is silent.

—*Traditional Jewish Prayer*

Do not despair; life wins.

—*Elie Wiesel*

Seek first the kingdom of God and
all else shall be added unto you.

—*Jesus*

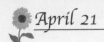

And the day came when the risk to remain
tight in a bud was more painful than the
risk it took to blossom.

—*Anaïs Nin*

The earth is the Lord's and the fullness thereof.

—from Psalm 24
(Hebrew Scriptures)

Teach your children what we have taught our children, that the earth is our mother. Whatever befalls the earth, befalls the children of the earth. If we spit upon the ground, we spit upon ourselves. This we know. The earth does not belong to us; we belong to the earth.

—Chief Seattle

Earth, with her thousand voices, praises God.

—Samuel Taylor Coleridge

An old guru and his disciple were on their way, about to cross a turbulent river, when they came upon a young woman standing paralyzed on the shore. Sensing her fear and desperation, the guru asked if they could be of service. The woman thanked him greatly, for although she was in great need of crossing the river, her fear of drowning had overwhelmed her. Immediately upon hearing this, the old guru lifted up the woman in his arms, took her safely to the other shore, and left her to go happily to her destination. The old guru and his disciple walked on in silence.

After some hours had passed, the young disciple abruptly cried out, "Tell me, my teacher, how did it feel to hold such a woman in your arms?" Almost breathlessly he went on, "Her lovely arms embracing you, her thighs wrapped around you, her sparkling eyes gazing into yours, her beautiful breasts brushing against your chest?"

The old guru was silent for a while. At last he turned to his disciple and said, "You are the one who knows how it feels to carry such a woman. I put her down hours ago at the riverbank, but you are still holding her."

—*Traditional Hindu Story*

It is one of the most beautiful compensations of this
life that no man can sincerely try to help another
without helping himself.

—*Ralph Waldo Emerson*

Try your best to treat others as you would wish
to be treated yourself, and you will find that
this is the shortest way to benevolence.

—*Mencius*

If you help others you will be helped, perhaps
tomorrow, perhaps in one hundred years,
but you will be helped.

—*George Gurdjieff*

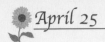

More than any other time in history, mankind
faces the crossroads. One path leads to despair and
utter hopelessness, the other to total extinction.
I pray we have the wisdom to choose wisely.

—*Woody Allen*

One of Master Bankei's students came to him and asked, "How can I get rid of my terrible anger?" Without pause, Bankei commanded, "Show it to me now." "I cannot just bring it out and show it to you," the student confessed. "It comes on its own without warning."

Bankei said, "Then it is not your true nature. If it were, it would always be with you."

—*Traditional Zen
Buddhist Story*

The fly cannot be driven away by getting angry at it.

—*West African Proverb*

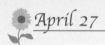

Believe nothing because a wise man said it.
Believe nothing because it is generally held.
Believe nothing because it is written.
Believe nothing because it is said to be divine.
Believe nothing because someone else believes it.
But believe only what you yourself judge to be true.

—Buddha

Overstraining is the enemy of accomplishment.
Calm strength that arises from a deep and
inexhaustible source is what brings success.

—*Rabindranath Tagore*

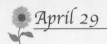

Like a lovely flower, full of color but lacking in fragrance, are the words of those who do not practice what they preach. Like a lovely flower full of color and fragrance are the words of those who practice what they preach.

The scent of flowers or sandalwood cannot travel against the wind; but the fragrance of the good spreads everywhere. Neither sandalwood nor the tagara flower, neither lotus nor jasmine, can come near the fragrance of the good.

—*from the Dhammapada*
(Sacred Book of Buddhism)

Before enlightenment, I chopped wood and carried water.
After enlightenment, I chopped wood and carried water.

—*Traditional Zen*
Buddhist Saying

If two angels were sent down from heaven—one to conduct an empire, and the other to sweep a street—they would feel no inclination to change employments.

—*Isaac Newton*

A dairymaid can milk cows to the glory of God.

—*Martin Luther*

He is enlightened who joins in this play knowing it as play, for man suffers only because he takes as serious what the gods made for fun.

—*Alan Watts*

Happiness is neither within us only, or without us;
it is the union of ourselves with God.

—*Pascal*

A happiness that is sought for ourselves alone can never
be found: for a happiness that is diminished by being
shared is not big enough to make us happy.

—*Thomas Merton*

One of the best ways to worship God is
simply to be happy.

—*Traditional Hindu
Saying*

A pious man came in lamentation to the great Rabbi Israel ben Eliezer, the one people called the Baal Shem Tov, the Master of the Good Name. His son had forsaken the religion of his people and the man was grief-stricken. "What shall I do, Rabbi?" cried the father. "Do you love your son?" the Baal Shem Tov asked. "Of course I do," said the man. "Then," said the rabbi, "love him even more."

—*Traditional Chassidic Jewish Story*

Even as the scent dwells within the flower,
so God resides always within your heart.

—*Traditional Sikh
Wisdom*

You are a second world in miniature; the sun and
moon are within you, and also the stars.

—*Origen*

If you wish to know the Divine, feel the wind on
your face and the warm sun on your hand.

—*Buddha*

That prayer has great power which a person makes with all his might. It makes a sour heart sweet, a sad heart merry, a poor heart rich, a foolish heart wise, a timid heart brave, a sick heart well, a blind heart full of sight, a cold heart ardent. It draws down the great God into the little heart; it drives the hungry soul up into the fullness of God; it brings together two lovers, God and the soul, in a wondrous place where they speak much of love.

—Mechtild of Magdeburg

Everyone prays in their own language, and there is
no language that God does not understand.

—Duke Ellington

Prayer enlarges the heart until it is capable
of containing God's gift of Himself.

—Mother Teresa

More things are wrought by prayer
Than this world dreams of.
Wherefore, let thy voice
Rise like a fountain for me night and day.

—Alfred, Lord Tennyson

Prayer does not change God, but it changes the one who prays.

—Sören Kierkegaard

A holy man named Aman made a journey to see the powerful Haroun Al-Rashid, the caliph who governed a great
empire. When Aman at last was allowed to see the caliph, the
simple man asked him a simple question: "If you were dying of
thirst and alone in the desert, what would you give for a single
cup of water?"

The caliph did not even pause for a moment. "I'd give half
my kingdom!" he shouted.

Aman nodded. Then quietly he asked, "And, what if the
water you drank somehow filled you up so much you were
about to burst? With your life in danger, O great Caliph, what
would you give for a few pills that would cure your condition
and keep your soul alive?"

"Surely I would give up the other half of my kingdom,"
Haroun Al-Rashid declared.

"Why then, O great Caliph," the saintly Aman inquired,
"do you talk about what fantastic worth your kingdom has
when you yourself are willing to give up the whole kingdom
for a mere cup of water and a handful of pills?"

—*Traditional Sufi Story*

A man came across the Buddha on the road one day and was awestruck. "Are you a god?" he asked. "No" was the reply. "Are you an immortal?" "No." "A holy saint?" Once again, the Buddha answered, "No." "Then," the man asked, "what are you?" The Buddha simply said, "I am awake."

—*Traditional Buddhist Story*

None are so old as those who have outlived enthusiasm.
—*Henry David Thoreau*

Once there was a man who was not only a very pious Jew, but also a student of the mystical Kabbala. Over the years, he had increased the time he devoted to prayer and holy invocations to the point where they occupied virtually the whole day. This poor man slept only a few hours each night, making certain not to miss either of the especially holy times for prayer to the Almighty, midnight and dawn. With all this, he expected to be showered with blessings, but instead he waxed poorer and poorer and found it difficult to support his family even in the most meager way. With his wife's encouragement, he went to see his teacher, a Kabbalistic master known for his great wisdom.

The rabbi heard the man's story and asked only, "What do you do the first thing in the morning?" The man answered truthfully, "I wash and purify myself for morning prayers. I prepare my ritual garments properly so as to make sure I am right before my God." And so he spoke, describing how he completed the morning prayers so righteously that it was well into the day before he began work, taking care of his animals and other tasks.

The rabbi said only, "Feed your chickens," and with that ended the meeting.

The poor man spent many a day pondering the mystical meaning of his rabbi's instructions, "Feed your chickens." Deciding it could

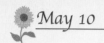
only mean that he had been lacking in truly nourishing his soul and that he needed to pray even more, he did just that. And, of course, his affairs (if it was possible) took a turn for the worse.

In desperation, he returned to the rabbi and told the master of his woes. Once again, the rabbi simply said, "Feed your chickens."

On the way home, the good man received a divine revelation. The rabbi meant exactly what he said: "Feed your chickens"—the real chickens his family kept to both eat and sell for profit.

The next morning he fed his chickens the very first thing, and from then on he prospered in all ways.

—Traditional Chassidic Jewish Story

In the beginner's mind, there are many possibilities.
In the expert's mind, there are few.

—*Shunryu Suzuki*

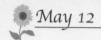

God could not be everywhere, so He made mothers.

—*Jewish Proverb*

The loveliest masterpiece of the heart of God
is the heart of a mother.

—*St. Thérèse of Lisieux*

Paradise is found at the feet of the mothers.

—*Muhammad*

He who stops completely before taking the next
step will spend a lifetime standing on one leg.

—*Chinese Proverb*

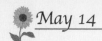

Things never go so well that one should have no fear,
and never so ill that one should have no hope.

—*Turkish Proverb*

If simply saying God's name brought liberation,
saying candy made your mouth sweet,
saying fire burned your feet,
saying water quenched your thirst,
saying food eliminated hunger,
the whole world would be free.

—*Kabir*

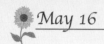

The Zen Master Ikkyu was clever even as a child. His master had a precious old teacup that one day Ikkyu mishandled and broke. He was standing there stunned, with the pieces of the cup in his hands, when he heard the footsteps of his teacher.

Instantly, Ikkyu put his hands behind his back and, seeing the master, asked, "Why do people have to die?" The master replied, "This is only natural. Everything has just so long to live and then it comes time to die." Ikkyu brought the broken teacup into view and said, "Dear Master, it was time for your cup to die."

—*Traditional Zen Buddhist Story*

How much more foolish are those who depend upon
words and seek understanding by their intellect!
They try to hit the moon with a stick.
They scratch their shoes when their feet itch.

—Wu-Men

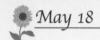

It is forbidden to live in a town
that does not have a green garden.

—from the Jerusalem Talmud
(Sacred Book of Judaism)

Ye are all leaves of one tree
and the fruits of one branch.

—*Bahá'u'lláh*

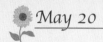
Every child is an idea of God.

—*Eberhard Arnold*

The child within us is simple and
daring enough to live the Secret.

—*Lao-tzu*

If you want to see the face of the Messiah,
just look at the children.

—*Rabbi Menachem
Mendel Schneerson*

A man was walking when he came upon a tiger. He ran, and the tiger chased him to the top of a cliff. The man grasped a wild vine and swung himself over the edge. As he hung suspended, the man heard the tiger above eagerly sniffing him. When he looked below, another hungry tiger awaited him. The man trembled, for only the thin vine kept him from the tigers' jaws.

Then two mice, a white one and a black one, began to nibble on the vine. The man saw right near him a delicious strawberry. Holding on tightly to the vine with one hand, the man snatched the strawberry with the other. How sweet it tasted!

—Traditional Zen Buddhist Story

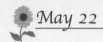
If for a moment we make way with our petty selves, wish no ill to anyone, apprehend no ill, cease to be but as a crystal which reflects a ray—what shall we not reflect! What a universe will appear crystallized and radiant around us.

—Henry David Thoreau

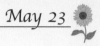
Never has a man who has made himself
crooked been able to make others straight.

—*Mencius*

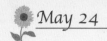

May the hand of a friend always be near to you and may
God fill your heart with gladness to cheer you.

—Traditional Irish Blessing

I want to be your friend
For ever and ever without break or decay.
When the hills are all flat
And the rivers are all dry,
When it lightens and thunders in winter,
When it rains and snows in summer,
When Heaven and Earth come together,
Not till then will I part from you.

—Ancient Chinese Oath

It is because one antelope will blow the dust from
the other's eye that two antelopes walk together.

—West African Proverb

Sometimes I go about pitying myself, and all the
time I am being carried on great winds across the sky.

> —*Traditional Ojibway Tribal Saying*
> *(Native American)*

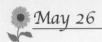 *May 26*

Our best chance of finding God is
to look in the place where we left him.

—*Meister Eckhart*

God often visits us, but most of
the time we are not at home.

—*French Proverb*

In sandy earth or deep
in valley soil I grow,
a wildflower thriving
on your love.

　　　　—from the Song of Songs
　　　　　(Hebrew Scriptures)

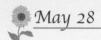
May 28

There is an ever-rotating wheel in this world. He who is rich today may not be so tomorrow, and he who is poor today may not be so tomorrow.

—*Traditional Jewish Saying*

Though the fig tree does not blossom,
nor fruit be on the vines,
the produce of the olive fail
and the fields yield no food,
the flock be cut off from the fold
and there be no herd in the stalls,
yet I will rejoice in the Lord.

*—from the Book of Habakkuk
(Hebrew Scriptures)*

This I know: the only way to live is like
the rose which lives without asking why.

—*Meister Eckhart*

The fragrance always remains
in the hand that gives the rose.

—*Gandhi*

The world was not left to us by our parents;
it was lent to us by our children.

—*African Proverb*

June 1

Wisdom is oftentimes nearer when
we stoop than when we soar.

—*William Wordsworth*

Nasreddin brought a bow and arrows with him to the country fair, and his students all came to see their teacher compete in the archery contest. Like all other contestants, Nasreddin was given three shots at the target. Before he took his first shot, Nasreddin put on the kind of hat a soldier wears and stood up very straight. Then he pulled the bow back hard and fired. Nasreddin missed the target completely, and the crowd laughed mightily at him.

Nasreddin picked up the bow once more and drew it back. This time he used much less strength, and although the arrow flew straight at the target, it fell far short.

Nasreddin only had his third shot left. He simply turned to face the target and fired the third arrow. It hit dead center, and the whole crowd went crazy! Everyone wanted to know how he made the last shot after not even having come close with the first two.

"I'll tell you," Nasreddin said. "For the first shot, I was imagining I was a soldier and a terrible enemy faced me. Fear caused the arrow to fly high over the target. When I took the second shot, I was thinking like a man who had missed his first one and was so nervous he could not concentrate. He was weak with worry, and the shot was weak, too."

Nasreddin paused. Finally a courageous soul spoke up. "And what about the third one? Who fired that arrow?"

"Oh," said Nasreddin. "That was me!"

—Traditional Sufi Story

One should follow the wise, the intelligent,
the learned, the much enduring, the dutiful, the noble;
one should follow a good and wise man, as the moon
follows the path of the stars.

—*Buddha*

A fox was crossing a river when the waters carried him away into the narrows and he became trapped. Seeing him helpless, a host of horseflies descended upon him.

After a long time, a wandering hedgehog came by and, out of sympathy for the miserable fox, asked him, "Would you like me to drive off those terrible flies for you?" The fox pleaded with the hedgehog to do nothing of the kind.

"But why not?" asked the hedgehog, very surprised.

"Because," the fox said, "the flies on me now have sucked for so long they are completely full. If you got rid of them, the new ones would take the very last drop of blood from my body!"

—Fable of Aesop

Dear God, be good to me.
The sea is so wide,
and my boat is so small.

—*Breton Fisherman's Prayer*

Love your enemies, for they tell you your faults.

—*Benjamin Franklin*

When we look deeply into the heart of a flower, we see clouds, sunshine, minerals, time, the earth, and everything else in the cosmos in it. Without clouds there could be no rain, and without rain there would be no flower.

—*Thich Nhat Hanh*

When I behold Your heavens, the work of Your fingers,
The moon and stars that You set in place:
What is man that You have been mindful of him,
Mortal man that You have taken note of him,
That You have made him little less than divine,
And adorned him with glory and majesty.

—*from Psalm 8*
(Hebrew Scriptures)

May all beings live happily and safe from harm
And may their hearts rejoice within themselves.
Whatever beings there may be with breath of life,
Whether they be weak or very strong,
Without exception, be they long or short,
Or middle-sized, or be they big or small,
Or thick, or visible, or invisible,
Or whether they dwell far or they dwell near,
Those that are here, those seeking to exist—
May all beings rejoice within themselves.
Let no one bring about another's ruin
And may none be despised in any way or place.
When provoked to animosity,
May no one wish ill of another being.

—from the Sutta Nipata
(Sacred Text of Buddhism)

It is better to suffer wrong than to do it,
and happier to be sometimes cheated than not to trust.

—*Samuel Johnson*

The Rabbi of Berdichev saw a man running down the street. He asked the man, "Why are you hurrying so?"

"I'm rushing to find my livelihood," the man answered.

"And how do you know," the rabbi asked, "that your livelihood is running ahead of you? Maybe it's behind you, and all you need to do is stop running and it will catch up to you."

—*Traditional Chassidic Jewish Story*

If a pickpocket meets a Holy Man,
he will see only his pockets.

—*Baba Hari Dass*

God is really only another artist. He invented the
giraffe, the elephant, the cat. He has no real style. He
just keeps on trying other things.

—*Pablo Picasso*

Be content with what you have;
rejoice in the way things are.
When you realize there is nothing lacking,
the whole world belongs to you.

—*Lao-tzu*

Angels can fly because they take themselves lightly.

—*G. K. Chesterton*

It is as if a king had sent you to a country to carry out one special, specific task. You go to the country and you perform a hundred other tasks, but if you have not performed the task you were sent for, it is as if you have done nothing at all. So man has come into the world for a particular task, and that is his purpose. If he doesn't perform it, he will have done nothing.

—*Rumi*

A man who is learning to use his eyes should begin by seeing a cartload of firewood; a man who is learning to use his ears should begin by hearing the clang of bells. Whenever there is ease within, there are no difficulties outside.

—from the Book of Lieh-tzu
(Classical Taoist Text)

Because you have made the Lord your refuge
The Most High your habitation,
No evil shall befall you
No scourge come near your tent

For he will give his angels charge of you
To guard you in all your ways.

—from Psalm 91
(Hebrew Scriptures)

God does not look at your forms and your possessions,
but He looks at your hearts and your deeds.

—*Muhammad*

Imagination is more important than knowledge.
—*Albert Einstein*

The man who has no imagination has no wings.
—*Muhammad Ali*

We can easily forgive a child who is afraid of the dark;
the real tragedy is when men are afraid of the light.

—*Plato*

When I am done thinking, I wander in the
woods gathering handfuls of flowers.

—Ryokan

The greatest revolution in our generation is the discovery
that human beings, by changing the inner attitudes of their
minds, can change the outer aspects of their lives.

—*William James*

There was a man who wandered throughout the world seeking the fulfillment of his deepest desires and the greatest of happiness. But in all his wanderings, he did not come to it. At last, tired from his arduous journey, he sat underneath a great tree at the foot of a mountain, which unbeknownst to him was The Great Wish-Fulfilling Tree.

As he rested beneath the tree, he thought, "It is so beautiful here. I wish I had a home on this very spot." And instantly, a lovely home appeared. The man was delightfully surprised, and he mused, "Ah, if only I had a wife to join me, then my happiness would be complete." And with that, a beautiful woman approached, calling him "my dear husband" and other such endearments. "First things first," he thought. "I am hungry, and I wish there was food to eat." And immediately a banquet table covered with the most exquisite dishes and delicacies appeared before the man. He hungrily began to feast, but, still tired, he thought, "I wish I had a servant to wait on me." The servant, too, promptly appeared.

His meal complete, the man leaned against the great tree, and thought, "How marvelous! Everything I wish for here comes true. There must be a mysterious power in this tree. I wonder if some kind of demon lives in it." And with that thought, a great demon came forth. "Oh," the man thought, "this demon will probably devour me!" And that is precisely what the demon did.

—Traditional Hindu Story

Do not think that love, in order to be genuine,
has to be extraordinary. What we need is to love
without getting tired.

—Mother Teresa

Where there is no love, pour love in,
and you will draw out love.

—St. John of the Cross

Some day, after mastering the winds, the waves,
the tides, and gravity, we shall harness for God the
energies of love, and then, for the second time in the
history of the world, man will have discovered fire.

—Pierre Teilhard de Chardin

There is nothing as easy as denouncing. It don't take much to see that something is wrong, but it takes some eyesight to see what will put it right again.

—*Will Rogers*

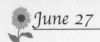 June 27

Advice is what we ask for when we already
know the answer but wish we didn't.

—Erica Jong

The moment one gives close attention to anything,
even a blade of grass, it becomes a mysterious, awesome,
indescribably magnificent world in itself.

—Henry Miller

Nasreddin planted a flower garden, but when the flowers came up so did a great crop of dandelions among them. Wishing to eliminate the unwanted guests, Nasreddin consulted with gardeners near and far, but none of their solutions worked.

Finally, Nasreddin traveled to the palace of the sheikh to seek the wisdom of the royal gardener himself. But alas, Nasreddin had already tried all the methods the kind old man recommended to him for eradicating such troublesome weeds.

Silently they sat together for a good long time. At last, the royal gardener looked at Nasreddin and said, "Well, then, the only thing I can suggest is that you learn to love them."

—Traditional Sufi Story

When love is strong, a man and woman can make their bed on a sword's blade. When love grows weak, a bed of sixty cubits is not large enough.

—*from the Babylonian Talmud*
(Sacred Book of Judaism)

The world is so empty if one thinks only of mountains, rivers and cities. But to know someone here and there who thinks and feels with us and who, though distant, is close to us in spirit, makes the earth for us an inhabited garden.

—Goethe

If a man is crossing a river, and an empty boat collides with his skiff, even though he be a bad-tempered man, he will not become very angry. But if he sees a man in the boat, he will shout at him to steer clear. If the shout is not heard, he will shout again, and yet again, and begin cursing. And all because there is somebody in the boat. Yet if the boat were empty, he would not be shouting, and not angry. If you can empty your own boat in crossing the river of the world, no one will oppose you, no one will seek to harm you.

—*Chuang-tzu*

Freedom is not worth having if it does not
include the freedom to make mistakes.

—*Gandhi*

A very good vision is needed for life and the man who has it must follow it—as the eagle seeks the deepest blue of the sky.

—*Chief Crazy Horse*

To be always talking is against nature. For the same reason a whirlwind never lasted a whole morning, nor a rainstorm all day. Who is it that makes the wind and rain? It is heaven and earth. And if even heaven and earth cannot blow or pour out for so long, how much less in his speaking should man?

—*from the Tao Te Ching*
(Sacred Book of Taoism)

The clearest way into the universe
is through a forest wilderness.

—*John Muir*

On a road among the eastern hills a Burmese traveler heard a Hillman shouting out his wares, which happened to be rice. But as he was shouting in his own language, the Burmese traveler did not understand and asked, "What is it? What is it?" The Hillman, of course, knew Burmese, but like most Hillmen, he spoke it with a twang. To enlighten the Burmese stranger, he shouted the Burmese word for rice.

The Burmese word for rice was *sunn*, but because of his twang, it sounded like *sinn*, which meant "elephant." So the Burmese traveler thought that the Hillman was warning him of an approaching wild elephant, and he started to run as fast as he could. The Hillman, although puzzled by the man's behavior, ran behind him. The sun was hot, and the road was rough. About an hour later the two arrived at a village, and both fainted through sheer exhaustion.

After the two strangers had been nursed back to consciousness, the villagers asked, "Why did you come running so hard? Did robbers waylay you, or did some wild animal chase you?" "This Hillman here warned me of an approaching wild elephant," explained the Burmese man. The Hillman looked at his fellow runner with amazement and denied that he had ever given such a warning. "Then why did *you* run?" the villagers asked. "It was quite simple," replied the Hillman. "I ran because he ran."

—*Traditional Burmese*
Buddhist Story

The young man who has not wept is a savage;
the old man who will not laugh is a fool.

—*George Santayana*

Deep peace
of the running wave to you,
Deep peace
of the quiet earth to you.
Deep peace
of the air to you,
Deep peace
of the shining star to you.

—*Celtic Christian Prayer Chant*

Just to be is a blessing.
Just to live is holy.

—*Rabbi Abraham Heschel*

A person will be called to account on judgment
day for every permissible thing that he
might have enjoyed but did not.

—*from the Jerusalem Talmud
(Sacred Book of Judaism)*

To try to extinguish the drive for riches with money is like
trying to quench a fire by pouring butterfat over it.

—*Hindu Proverb*

Money can buy the husk of many things, but not the kernel.
It brings you food, but not appetite; medicine, but not health;
acquaintances, but not friends; days of joy,
but not peace and happiness.

—*Henrik Ibsen*

Money has never yet made anyone rich.

—*Seneca*

Master Tanzan, on the day of his death, called upon his assistant to send a batch of identical postcards. Each one said simply: "I am departing this world. There will be no further messages. Tanzan."

—*Traditional Zen Buddhist Story*

In the face of an obstacle which is impossible
to overcome, stubbornness is stupid.

—*Simone de Beauvoir*

I tell you the truth, if you have faith as small as
a mustard seed, you can say to this mountain,
Move from here to there, and it will move.
Nothing will be impossible for you.

—*Jesus*

In spite of everything I still believe that
people are really good at heart.

—Anne Frank

What if you slept? And what if in your sleep, you dreamed? And what if in your dream you went to heaven and there plucked a strange and beautiful flower? And what if when you awoke, you had the flower in your hand? Ah! What then?

—*Samuel Taylor Coleridge*

On his early morning walk along the shore, an old man noticed a young woman picking up starfish and tossing them into the ocean. As they passed each other, the old man said, "Pardon me, but why are you picking up all those starfish?" The young woman answered, "Because if I leave them stranded, they'll die in the hot sun."

"But," the old man said, "this beach is miles long and there must be millions of starfish on it. No matter how many you rescue, how can it make any difference?"

The young woman looked down at the starfish in her hands, threw it into the sea, and said: "It makes a difference to this one."

—*Contemporary Spiritual Story*

God is an angel in an angel, and a stone in a stone,
and a straw in a straw.

—*John Donne*

The distance between you and God is
as thin as an insect's wing.

—*from the Guru Granth Sahib
(Sacred Sikh Scripture)*

The world is charged with the grandeur of God.

—*Gerard Manley Hopkins*

Grant me the ability to be alone;
may it be my way every day to go outdoors
among the trees and grasses,
among all growing things,
and there may I be alone,
to talk with the one
that I belong to.

—*Prayer of Rabbi Nachman
of Bratzlav*

In a small hut, Hakuin lived a quiet life devoted to monastic purity. When the young unmarried daughter of the village grocer became pregnant, she named Hakuin as the father. Her outraged parents went to Hakuin and charged him with the deed. Hakuin simply said, "Is that so?"

When the child was born, once again the parents came to Hakuin. They handed him the baby and demanded he take responsibility for raising it. Hakuin said, "Is that so?" and took the baby in his arms. Dutifully, he began to look after the infant.

A year later, the young woman could bear it no longer. She confessed that the real father was a young man who worked in the nearby fishmarket. The parents went to Hakuin once more, this time making deep apologies, and asked him to return the child. Hakuin said only, "Is that so?" and gave the baby back to them.

—*Traditional Zen Buddhist Story*

A troubled mother took her daughter to see Mahatma
Gandhi, who was world-renowned for his great spiritual disci-
pline. It seems the young girl had become addicted to eating
sweets, and her mother wanted Gandhi to speak to her about
this harmful habit and convince her to drop it. Upon hearing
the request, Gandhi paused in silence and then told the
mother, "Bring the girl back to me in three weeks and I will
speak to her then."

Just as she was instructed, the mother returned with her
daughter, and Gandhi, as he had promised, spoke to the girl
about the detrimental effects of eating too many sweets. He
counseled her to give them up.

The mother gratefully thanked Gandhi, but was perplexed.
"Why," she asked him, "did you not speak to my daughter
when first we came to you?"

"My good woman," Gandhi replied, "three weeks ago I
myself was still addicted to sweets!"

—*Story of Gandhi*

Generosity is not in giving me that which I need
more than you do, but it is in giving me that which
you need more than I do.

—*Kahlil Gibran*

The little that one produces oneself with a broken
hoe is better than the plenty that another gives you.

—*West African Proverb*

Fear less, hope more; eat less, chew more; whine less, breathe more; talk less, say more; hate less, love more; and all good things are yours.

—*Swedish Proverb*

The stick that is at your friend's house
will not drive away the leopard.

—*Central African Proverb*

Chuang-tzu had a dream, and when he woke up this is what he said: "I, Chuang-tzu, dreamed that I was a butterfly, flying here and there. I thought only of things a butterfly takes a fancy to and thought about none of the things a man like myself does. Suddenly I woke up. There I was, Chuang-tzu, the man, once more. Now I do not know if I am a man dreaming I was a butterfly or if I am a butterfly dreaming I am a man!"

—*Traditional Taoist Story*

The clouds above us come together and disperse;
The breeze in the courtyard departs and returns.
Life is like that, so why not relax?
Who can keep us from celebrating?

—*Lu-Yu*

As the bee takes the essence of the flower and
flies without destroying its beauty and perfume,
so wander in this life.

—*Buddha*

July 29

The body is the soul's house. Shouldn't we therefore
take care of our house so that it doesn't fall into ruin?

—*Philo Judaeus*

When you make the two one, and when you make
the inner as the outer and the outer as the inner
and the above as the below, and when you make
the male and female into a single one—then shall
you enter the Kingdom.

—*Jesus*

The origin of all trouble
Within this world
Is a single word
Spoken in haste.

—*from the Moritake Arakida*
(Classical Shinto Text)

Be patient toward all that is unsolved in your
heart and learn to love the questions themselves,
like locked rooms and like books that
are written in a very strange language.

—*Rainer Maria Rilke*

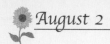

And now, may kindly Columba guide you
To be an isle in the sea,
To be a hill on the shore,
To be a star in the night,
To be a staff for the weak.

—*Traditional Celtic Prayer*

A man should not breed a savage dog,
nor place a shaking ladder in his house.

—*Jewish Proverb*

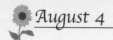

It is a funny thing about life:
If you refuse to accept anything but
the best you very often get it.

—*Somerset Maugham*

Do not tell tales about either friends or enemies. Unless silence makes you an accomplice, never betray a secret. Have you heard a rumor? Let it die with you. Never fear, it will not make you burst.

A fool with a secret goes through agony like a woman in childbirth.

—*Wisdom of Ben Sira*
(Sacred Book of Judaism)

A pious nun made a beautiful golden statue of Buddha which she kept with her on all her journeys. After many years, she came to live in a small country temple where there were numerous altars, each with its own statue of Buddha.

The nun desired to worship only before her golden Buddha, so when she lit incense, she fashioned a funnel to direct the smoke to it—and not to any of the others. In just a short time, the face of the golden Buddha became black and ugly.

—*Traditional Zen Buddhist Story*

Out beyond fields of wrongdoing and rightdoing,
there is a field. I will meet you there.

—Rumi

Integrity is so perishable in the summer months of success.

—_Vanessa Redgrave_

A poor and troubled man came to Kotzk to see his rabbi and ask his help. "Do not worry," the rabbi told him. "Pray with all your heart and surely God will hear and be merciful to you."

The man said, "But Rabbi, I do not know how to pray." The rabbi's heart filled with pity. "In that case," he said, "you really do have a lot to worry about."

—*Traditional Chassidic Jewish Story*

God fits the back to the burden.

—*Scottish Proverb*

Be a gardener, dig a ditch, toil and sweat, and turn the earth upside down and seek the deepness and water the plants in time. Continue this labor and make sweet floods to run and noble and abundant fruits to spring. Take this food and drink and carry it to God as your true worship.

—*Julian of Norwich*

I would rather be ashes than dust, I would rather that my spark should burn out in a brilliant blaze than it should be stifled by dry rot. I would rather be a superb meteor, every atom in me in magnificent glow, than a sleepy and permanent planet.

—*Jack London*

The perfect man is a spiritual being. Were the ocean itself scorched up, he would not be hot. Were the Milky Way frozen hard, he would not feel cold. Were the mountains to be shaken by thunder, and the great deep to be tossed up by storm, he would not tremble in such case; he would mount upon the clouds of heaven and, driving the sun and the moon before him, pass beyond the limits of this world, where death and life hold no more power over man.

—*Chuang-tzu*

Think of Divine Abundance as a mighty, refreshing rain. Whatever receptacle you have at hand will receive it. If you hold up a tin cup, you will receive only that quantity. If you hold up a bowl, that will be filled. What kind of receptacle are you holding up to Divine Abundance?

—*Paramahansa Yogananda*

A lion fell in love with the daughter of a farmer and asked permission to marry her. The farmer was not pleased with the idea of his daughter marrying such an awful beast, but was not happy, to say the least, with the prospect of rejecting the lion either.

So the farmer took the lion aside and told him that he approved the marriage, but that his daughter, understandably, was trembling with fear. If the lion would agree to have his long, sharp teeth and terrible claws removed, the farmer would then give his consent.

The lion was so enamored of his beloved that he agreed. But when he returned, toothless and clawless, to claim his bride, he was met with laughter and ridicule. Then, with nothing but a stick, he was chased off back to the forest.

—Fable of Aesop

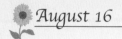

Of all that God has shown me
I can speak just the smallest word,
Not more than a honey bee
Takes on his foot
From an overflowing jar.

—*Mechtild of Magdeburg*

Master Soyen Shaku was known as one who never wasted a moment. Though he was a tough taskmaster, especially on himself, he allowed his students to sleep on hot summer days.

When Master Soyen Shaku was but a boy of twelve, he was already studying very deep questions. He talked to the older monks as if he were a monk himself.

One summer day, while his teacher was away, Soyen became so sleepy in the stuffy air that he lay down near the doorway and napped. Three hours later, little Soyen suddenly woke up. His master had come back!

But it was too late to move. There he was on the floor, and the master was opening the door.

"I beg your pardon," Soyen's master said, as he most carefully stepped over his little student's body. "I beg your pardon."

Soyen never slept in the afternoon again.

—Traditional Zen Buddhist Story

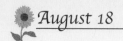

When it is dark enough, you can see the stars.

—*Ralph Waldo Emerson*

When an arrow is released from the bow, it may go straight, or it may not, according to what the archer does.

How strange, therefore, that when the arrow flies straight, it is due to the skill of the archer, but when it goes amiss, it is the arrow which receives the curses!

—Attar

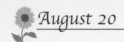

Even at the venerable age of eighty, Master Hyakujo worked alongside his students on the monastery grounds. He gardened, pruned trees, and cleaned just as younger monks did. They dared not ask him to stop, so the students, not wishing to see their old master work so hard, hid his tools.

That day the master did not eat. He did not eat the next day, nor the one after. The students thought, "Perhaps the master is angry at missing his tools," and so the students returned them to their proper place.

That day the master worked and ate his food as always. In the evening, he gave a simple teaching: "No work, no food."

—*Traditional Zen Buddhist Story*

Our minds are like crows. They pick up everything that glitters, no matter how uncomfortable
our nests get with all that metal in them.

—*Thomas Merton*

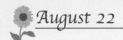

When a man begins to call on the sacred name,
a lotus flower begins to grow in Paradise for him.

—Fa-Chao

One cannot help but be in awe when he contemplates the mysteries of eternity, of life, of the marvelous structure of reality. It is enough if one tries merely to comprehend a little of this mystery every day. Never lose a holy curiosity.

—*Albert Einstein*

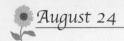

Why was Adam created on the sixth day, after all the other creatures?

So that should a person become prideful, he may be reminded that the gnats preceded him in the order of creation.

—from the Babylonian Talmud
(Sacred Book of Judaism)

I am not going to die.
I'm going home like a shooting star.

—*Sojourner Truth*

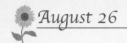

Some children were playing by a river making sand castles. Each one built his own and defended it, saying, "It's mine." When all the castles were finished, one child kicked over another one's, completely destroying it. The castle owner flew into a rage, punched the offender in the face, and pulled his hair. "He has ruined my castle," the child shouted to the others. "Come help me give him what he deserves."

The children beat the one who had knocked over the castle, and they stomped on him too. Then they went back to play with their own castles, each one saying, "This castle is mine; don't touch it!"

After a while, it began to get dark and the children thought they ought to be going home. No one cared about the sand castles anymore. One child trampled on his and another pushed his over with his hands. Then they all turned away and went home.

—*Traditional Buddhist Story*

I am a little pencil in the hand of a writing God
who is sending a love letter to the world.

—*Mother Teresa*

May our walking on earth be gentle as
the union of the butterfly and the flower.

—*Traditional Buddhist Blessing*

People are afraid when dark clouds gather and thunder clashes. But clouds and thunder are nothing; they are only the sources of rain for the hot and parched earth. Do not be afraid of clouds; do not be afraid of difficulties. Keep moving straight ahead. Give your hand to God, and He will keep you in the light twenty-four hours a day.

—*Baba Virsa Singh*

It is not because things are difficult that we do not dare;
it is because we do not dare that they are difficult.

—*Seneca*

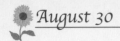

How beautiful it is to do nothing,
and then rest afterward.

—*Spanish Proverb*

What else can I do, a lame old man, but sing hymns to God? If I were a nightingale, I would do the nightingale's part; if I were a swan, I would do as a swan. But now I am a rational creature, and I ought to praise God. This is my work. I do it, nor will I desert my post, so long as I am allowed to keep it. And I ask you to join me in this same song.

—Epictetus

A man hoping to find wisdom traveled to Poland to see the renowned Rabbi Hafez Hayyim. When he arrived at the celebrated rabbi's house, he was surprised to see that it was nothing more than a room. There, the rabbi sat on a bench at a small table surrounded only by the numerous volumes of books he continually pored over in study.

The seeker asked, "Good Rabbi, where are all your belongings? Where are your furnishings?"

Hafez answered, "Tell me, where are yours?"

"Where are mine?" said the startled man. "But I only came here for a short visit."

"So did I," the rabbi said.

—*Traditional Chassidic Jewish Story*

Rajah Koranya had a king banyan tree called Steadfast, and the shade of its widespread branches was cool and lovely. No one guarded the tree, and no one hurt another for its fruit. Now there came a man who ate his fill of fruit, broke down a branch, and went his way. Thought the spirit dwelling in that tree, "How amazing, how astonishing it is, that a man should be so evil as to break off a branch of the tree, after eating his fill. Suppose the tree were to bear no more fruit." And the tree bore no more fruit.

—*Traditional Buddhist Story*

Teach us, Lord, to accept our limitations.
It is of great advantage that we shall know our place,
and not imagine that the whole universe exists for us alone.

—Moses Maimonides

God respects me when I work,
but loves me when I sing.

—*Rabindranath Tagore*

One day, King Shavaji's great elephant ran amok, destroying everything in his path. As it so happened, the village know-it-all was just then returning from a lecture, completely unaware of the rampaging elephant coming his way. The villagers tried to warn the man, but he dismissed their fears for his safety. "Look, you ignorant fools," he snorted. "Don't you know that you must see the God Rama in everything? Have you no spiritual understanding? Rama is in all things and creatures, so what do I care about an elephant? Remember to see Rama in everything."

The people thought the man as mad as the elephant, but as he would not listen they let him go. When he came upon the elephant, it lifted the man up like a stick and dashed him on some rocks. Then the elephant picked him up and threw him down several times more. Somehow the elephant was seized while the man still had life in him.

After a long time he recovered from his injuries and went to have a word with his teacher. "Look here," he argued, "you told me that Rama is all there is. I believed that the elephant was Rama, and it almost killed me."

The teacher answered: "You fool. Why couldn't you see Rama in the people who told you to stay clear of the elephant?"

—*Traditional Hindu Story*

All ambitions are lawful except those which climb
upward on the miseries or credulities of mankind.

—*Joseph Conrad*

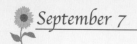

On Rosh Hashanah, the Rabbi of Berdichev sought the most righteous person to blow the sacred ram's horn. Blowing the shofar was the sign that the New Year had begun and all were to prepare for the upcoming Day of Atonement.

As each candidate came forward, the rabbi asked, "What holy thoughts will you be thinking when you blow the shofar?" But no one's answer satisfied him. Finally, a man approached who said that he was ignorant of holy teaching and had no great and lofty thoughts. "Then what is it you will be thinking as you blow the shofar?" asked the rabbi.

"I'll be thinking about my four unmarried daughters and how they are to find husbands. I'll say to God, 'I'm doing my duty by You, now You do your duty by me.'"

He was the one chosen to blow the shofar.

—*Traditional Chassidic Jewish Story*

Let those who have need of more ask for it humbly.
And let those who have need of less thank God.

—*St. Benedict*

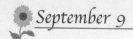

If you meditate on your ideal,
you will acquire its nature.
If you think of God day and night,
you will acquire the nature of God.

—*Ramakrishna*

It is glory enough for me
That I should be Your servant.

It is grace enough for me
That You should be my Lord.

> —*Traditional Muslim Prayer*

Treat people and live amongst them in such a way
so that when you die they will cry over you, and
while you are alive they long for your company.

—*Traditional Muslim Saying*

He who has a thousand friends has not a friend to spare,
and he who has one enemy will meet him everywhere.

—*Ali*

Pray for your enemies, that they may be holy and that all
may be well with them. And should you think this is not
serving God, rest assured that more than all prayers, this
is indeed the service of God.

—*from the Talmud*
(Sacred Book of Judaism)

The prophet Muhammad (peace be upon him) was teaching, reciting the Qur'an to an assembly of earnest listeners out on the desert sands not too far from their tents, when a sickly cat walked straight up to Muhammad (peace be upon him), sat down on the hem of his exquisite and precious robe, and went to sleep.

All day the prophet Muhammad (peace be upon him) spoke and conversed with the believers, the sun rising to its fullest and falling again, and none of the party nor the prophet Muhammad (peace be upon him) stirred. The cat as well remained asleep and still, healing the way cats do in the protection of the prophet Muhammad (peace be upon him) and the succor of his robe.

At last, the day was coming to its end, and all, as well as the prophet Muhammad (peace be upon him), were now to return to their dwelling places for the night. Without a word, the prophet Muhammad (peace be upon him) took a knife, cut off the hem of his robe on which the sick cat still lay sleeping, by this act destroying the finest of robes, and left the cat undisturbed.

—*Traditional Muslim Story*

I am a creature of God and my neighbor is also a creature of God.
I work in the city and he works in the country.
I rise early for my work and he rises early for his work.
Just as he cannot excel in my work, I cannot excel in his work.
Will you say that I do great things and he does small things?
We have learned that it does not matter
whether a person does much or little
As long as he directs his heart to heaven.

—*from the Babylonian Talmud*
(Sacred Book of Judaism)

Let nothing frighten you.
Everything is changing;
God alone is changeless.
Patience achieves the aim.
Who has God lacks nothing;
God alone fills all needs.

—*Prayer of St. Teresa of Avila*

Where there is forgiveness,
there is God Himself.

> —*from the Adi Granth*
> *(Sacred Sikh Text)*

A man went to the same house of prayer as the holy Baal Shem Tov. However, he never brought his simple-minded son with him, for the boy had not learned to read from a prayer book.

When the boy turned thirteen and was to be a full-fledged member of the community, the father decided at last to take him to worship on Yom Kippur, the Holiest of Holy Days. But without his father's knowledge, the boy slipped his little shepherd's flute into his pocket just before they left home.

All through the service, for hour after hour the boy sat perfectly still and quiet. But when the additional holiday service began, the boy asked if he now could play his flute. His father angrily told him to hush. When the boy persisted, the father clasped his hand over the boy's pocket to stop him from getting out his flute.

At last, the Closing Service began. The boy suddenly grabbed his father's hand away, pulled out his flute, and blew mightily into it. The worshipers were horrified, but the Baal Shem Tov, without pause, went on with the service.

Afterward, the Baal Shem Tov revealed that it was only because the boy played his flute that the congregation's prayers had been carried up to heaven.

—*Traditional Chassidic Jewish Story*

A poor man scraped together just enough money to buy an old run-down farm. The very next day he began to make improvements on the neglected property. After two years of hard work and good management, the farm began to prosper. Having caught wind of the farmer's good fortune, the village priest showed up. "Well, neighbor," he declared, "God be praised, for He has done wonders with your farm." "Pardon me, Father," retorted the man, "but you should have seen the farm when it was in God's hands."

—*Contemporary Spiritual Story*

God is our refuge and strength,
a very present help in trouble.
Therefore we will not fear, though the earth should change,
though the mountains shake in the heart of the sea;
though its waters roar and foam,
though the mountains tremble with its tumult.

There is a river whose streams make glad the city of God,
the holy habitation of the Most High.
God is in the midst of the city; it shall not be moved;
God will help it when the morning dawns.

—*from Psalm 46*
(Hebrew Scriptures)

Children begin by loving their parents;
as they grow older they judge them;
sometimes they forgive them.

—*Oscar Wilde*

Though a tree grow ever so high,
the falling leaves still return to the ground.

—*Malay Proverb*

The Mullah Nasreddin had been saving his money for a long time to buy a new shirt. At last he had enough, and full of excitement, he went to the tailor's shop to place his order. The tailor took the mullah's measurements and, that completed, told him: "Come back in a week and—*Insh'allah*, as God wills it—your shirt will be done and waiting for you."

Nasreddin, keeping to this agreement, returned, to the hour, one week later and asked for his new shirt. "Something has come up," the tailor informed the poor mullah. "Your shirt is not yet finished, but—*Insh'allah*, as God wills it—tomorrow your shirt will be ready."

Still hopeful, Nasreddin returned the next day. "I'm sorry, Mullah," the tailor apologized, "but it's still not quite ready. Try again tomorrow and—*Insh'allah*, as God wills it—it will be ready."

"How long then will it take," Nasreddin inquired this time, "if you leave Allah out of it altogether?"

—*Traditional Sufi Story*

The beauty of the trees,
the softness of the air,
the fragrance of the grass,
speaks to me.

The summit of the mountain,
the thunder of the sky,
the rhythm of the sea,
speaks to me.

The faintness of the stars,
the freshness of the morning,
the dewdrop on the flower,
speaks to me.

The strength of the fire,
the taste of salmon,
the trail of the sun,
and the life that never goes away,
they speak to me.
And my heart soars.

—*Chief Dan George*

Never try to teach a pig to sing.
It wastes your time and annoys the pig.

—*Mark Twain*

Be kind: Everyone you meet is fighting a hard battle.

—*John Watson*

Those who act kindly in this world will have kindness.

—*from the Qur'an*
(Holy Book of Islam)

My religion is very simple—my religion is kindness.

—*Dalai Lama*

King Solomon wanted to build a great temple for people to pray to God. He wanted to build on the holiest of places in all Israel, but what spot was that?

One night, it is said, Solomon took a long walk in the fields. He saw a man carrying heavy sacks of wheat, one after the other, from one barn to another nearby. Then the man slipped away into the dark night. "He must be a thief," Solomon thought, but he decided to keep watching.

Soon a different man appeared. He did the same thing, only he carried the sacks of wheat back to the original barn! Then he, too, left in silence.

The next day Solomon commanded the first man to see him. "Why do you steal wheat from your neighbor in the middle of the night?" he asked him.

The man replied, "I do not steal. My neighbor is my brother. He has a wife and many children to feed, while I do not. He needs much more than I do, but he won't take any extra wheat from me. So every night I secretly carry wheat from my barn to his."

Then Solomon asked the other man to come and asked him why he took wheat from his barn and put it in another. The man answered, "I have the help of my whole family, but my brother has none. He has to pay for help, and so he needs more wheat. He won't

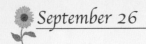
take it from me, so in the night I secretly give the wheat to him."

Solomon brought the two men together and told them what each of them had done. "No wonder my pile of wheat sacks always stays the same," they both said, and laughed. And then they embraced each other with a hug full of love!

Solomon said, "Now I know the holiest place in all Israel! It is your land, where brothers love each other this much. So the temple shall be built here!"

—*Traditional Jewish Story*

Oh Great Spirit, whose voice I hear in the winds, life to all the world, hear me: I come before you, one of your many children. I am small and weak. I need your strength and wisdom. Let me walk in beauty and make my eyes ever behold the red and purple sunset. Make my hands respect the things you have made, my ears sharp to hear your voice. Make me wise, so that I may know the things you have taught my people, the lesson you have hidden in every leaf and rock. I seek strength not to be superior to my brothers, but to be able to fight my greatest enemy—myself.

Make me ever ready to come to you with clean hands and straight eyes, so when life fades as a fading sunset, my spirit may come to you without shame.

—*Prayer of Chief Yellow Lark*

There are seven kinds of offering that can be practiced by even those who are not wealthy. The first is the physical offering. This is to offer service by one's labor. The highest type of this offering is to offer one's own life. The second is the spiritual offering. This is to offer a compassionate heart to others. The third is the offering of eyes. This is to offer a warm glance to others, which will give them tranquillity. The fourth is the offering of countenance. This is to offer a soft countenance with a smile to others. The fifth is the speech offering. This is to offer kind and warm words to others. The sixth is the seat offering. This is to offer one's seat to others. The seventh is the offering of shelter. This is to let others spend the night at one's home. These kinds of offering can be practiced by anyone in everyday life.

—Buddha

If we are to achieve greatness and a name celebrated
all over the earth, but find not favor with the Lord,
what would it all be worth?

—*Guru Nanak*

May the blessed sunlight shine upon you
and warm your heart
till it glows like a great fire
and strangers may warm themselves
as well as friends.
And may the light shine out of the eyes of you,
like a candle set in the window of a house,
bidding the wanderer to come in
out of the storm.

—Traditional Irish Blessing

Go slowly and you shall surely arrive.
—*Milarepa*

Verily I say unto you, whosever shall not receive the
kingdom of God as a little child, he shall not enter therein.

—Jesus

If we are to reach real peace in the world,
we shall have to begin with children.

—Gandhi

Let us put our minds together and see
what we will make for our children.

—Chief Sitting Bull

Rabbi Safra was saying his morning prayers when a customer came to buy his donkey, so he did not respond when the buyer made his offer. Taking the rabbi's silence as a rejection, the man upped the price. When the rabbi remained silent, the buyer substantially added to his bid. But Rabbi Safra remained in prayer.

After the rabbi finished, he said to the buyer, "I had decided to sell you my donkey at the first price you spoke of, but I did not want to interrupt my prayers to talk to you. So, you may have the donkey at that price—any other offers I will not accept."

—Aha of Shabha

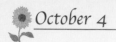

Let us know peace.
For as long as the moon shall rise,
For as long as the rivers shall flow,
For as long as the sun will shine,
For as long as the grass shall grow,
Let us know peace.

—*Traditional Tis-Tsis-Tas/*
Cheyenne Tribal Prayer
(Native American)

Some of your hurts you have cured
And the sharpest you've even survived,
But what torments of grief you've endured
From evils which never arrived.

—*Ralph Waldo Emerson*

I never think of the future. It comes soon enough.

—*Albert Einstein*

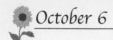

When a man suffers he ought not to say, "That's bad!"
Nothing that God imposes on man is bad. But, it is all right
to say, "That's bitter!" For among medicines there
are some made with bitter herbs.

—*Traditional Chassidic Jewish Saying*

You never know what is enough unless
you know what is more than enough.

—*William Blake*

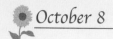

Consider the flame of a single lamp. Though a hundred thousand people come and light their own lamps from it so that they can cook their food and ward off the darkness, the first lamp remains the same as before. Blessings are like this, too.

—Buddha

When one who has a true hold on life walks on land he does not meet tigers or wild buffaloes. In battle, he is not touched by weapons of war. Indeed, a buffalo that attacked him would find nothing for his horns to butt, a tiger would find nothing for its claws to tear, a weapon would find no place for its blade to lodge.

—*from the Tao Te Ching*
(Sacred Book of Taoism)

The time of business does not with me differ from the time of prayer, and in the noise and clatter of my kitchen, while several persons are at the same time calling for different things, I possess God in as great tranquility as if I were upon my knees at the blessed sacrament.

—*Brother Lawrence*

You have made us for yourself, and our hearts are restless, until they rest in you.

—*St. Augustine*

You must always do the thing you think you cannot do.
—*Eleanor Roosevelt*

You are to be a wanderer, coming to and going from strange villages. It may be that you accomplish nothing in any of those places. It may be that the goods you carry to trade are not found favorable anywhere.

Do not turn back; keep your step strong. You will accomplish that which the Master of the Universe gives you to do.

—*Chilam Balam*

Wonder rather than doubt is the root of knowledge.

—*Rabbi Abraham Heschel*

Spiritual knowledge is like water:
It takes the color and shape of the cup.

—*Shah Naqshband*

If one is not oneself a sage or saint, the best thing
one can do is to study the words of those who were.

—*Aldous Huxley*

Trees and stones will teach you that which
you can never learn from masters.

—*St. Bernard of Clairvaux*

It is possible to fly without motors,
but not without knowledge and skill.

—*Wilbur Wright*

I am still learning.

—*Michelangelo*

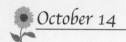

One day a farmer went out from his farm. He closed the gate to the yard where all the animals stayed, meaning to return in a short while. But days and days went by and the farmer did not come back. All the animals became very hungry and thirsty. Even the rooster lost the energy to crow.

The animals sat motionless in the shade of a big tree, trying to stay alive until the farmer gave them food and water again. But the peacock gathered all his remaining strength together. He rose up, opened his multicolored tail, and strutted before all the other animals.

"Mama," asked a little chicken, "why is the peacock showing off his tail like that?"

"Because the peacock is so proud of the way he looks," she answered. "My child, this is a fault that will only disappear with death."

—*Fable of Leonardo da Vinci*

Laughter is the language of the soul.

—*Pablo Neruda*

I am especially glad of the divine gift of laughter:
it has made the world human and lovable,
despite all its pain and wrong.

—*W. E. B. DuBois*

If you're not allowed to laugh in Heaven,
I don't want to go there.

—*Martin Luther*

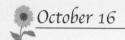

The wise man in the storm prays to God,
not for safety from danger, but for deliverance from fear.
It is the storm within which endangers him,
not the storm without.

—Ralph Waldo Emerson

The only thing we have to fear is fear itself.

—Franklin D. Roosevelt

Keep your fears to yourself; share your courage with others.

—Robert Louis Stevenson

In their freedom, birds make
Expanding circles in the sky.
How do they learn to be free?
They fall—and by falling
Are given wings to fly.

—*Rumi*

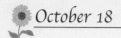

An elderly Chinese martial arts master who could still toss around eight of his best students simultaneously was asked, "If you were accosted by a gunman in an alley, what would you do?" "Run like hell," he replied.

—*Contemporary Spiritual Anecdote*

A gentle hand may lead an elephant with a single hair.
                                        —*Persian Proverb*

Hold on to what is good
Even if it is a handful of earth.
Hold on to what you believe
Even if it is a tree which stands by itself.
Hold on to what you must do
Even if it is a long way from here.
Hold on to life
Even when it is easier letting go.
Hold on to my hand
Even when I have gone away from you.

—*Traditional Tewa/Pueblo Tribal Wisdom*
(Native American)

Not in entire forgetfulness,
And not in utter nakedness,
But trailing clouds of glory do we come
From God who is our home.

—*William Wordsworth*

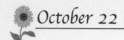

Turn yourself into gold and then live wherever you please.
—*Ramakrishna*

A rock pile ceases to be a rock pile the
moment a single man contemplates it,
bearing within him the image of a cathedral.

—*Antoine de Saint Exupéry*

October 24

When spider webs unite, they can tie up a lion.
—Ethiopian Proverb

Arriving at the marketplace, a poor priest, dressed in rags, begged for a pear from a rich farmer. Instead, the busy farmer cursed the priest for pestering him. The market guard, seeing the large crowd getting upset at the farmer's refusal, bought a single pear himself and gave it to the priest. The humble priest thanked the guard, turned to the crowd, and announced, "Please allow me to offer some fragrant pears to all of you."

"But you have only one yourself," they said, "and no money to buy more."

"I need only one," he replied, then proceeded to gobble up the precious pear and removed a single seed from its core. The priest took this seed, quickly dug a small hole, and planted it. He asked for a large bucket of hot water and poured it over the pear seed.

Behold! A tiny seedling appeared. In what seemed like just a brief moment, it became a full-grown tree laden with masses of ripe, golden pears. The priest calmly picked the luscious fruits, presented them to the people, and, his promise fulfilled, walked on.

—*Traditional Taoist Story*

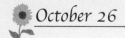

Useless is a great yield of milk
From a cow that kicks the pail over.

—*Muhammad Muinuddin Chishti*

My heart stands in waiting and hope as the trees
stand still through the darkness of night.

—*Hazrat Inayat Khan*

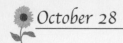

Nothing in this world can take the place of persistence. Talent will not; nothing is more common than unsuccessful men with great talent. Genius will not; unrewarded genius is almost a proverb. Education will not; the world is full of educated derelicts. Persistence, determination alone are omnipotent.

—*Ray Kroc*

How do geese know when to fly to the sun? Who tells them the seasons? How do we, humans, know when it is time to move on? As with the migrant birds, so surely with us, there is a voice within, if only we would listen to it, that tells us so certainly when to go forth into the unknown.

—*Elisabeth Kübler-Ross*

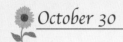

The one known as the Laughing Buddha lived as a poor monk in the monastery of Fenghua. He always had a bag with him, even when eating or sleeping, so everyone called him the Monk with the Bag.

One day, the God of Fire came to visit the temple and reduced it to ashes. The abbot ordered the Monk with the Bag to collect offerings to rebuild the temple, and in obedience he set off with his bag. After many days of wandering, he arrived at the house of a widow who owned an entire mountain covered with tall trees, most of which had not been touched in over a hundred years.

The Monk with the Bag begged the widow to let him fill his bag with her trees, and thinking he was making a joke, she gave him her permission. The monk employed some foresters, cut down every tree on the mountain, and put them all in his bag.

When she saw what had happened, the widow was shocked. She knelt down before the Monk with the Bag, but he said, "Do not kneel. You have made your offering." And smiling, he added, "In just three years, you will have all your trees once more."

—*Traditional Chinese Buddhist Story*

We ourselves cannot put any magic spell on this world.
The world is its own magic.

—*Shunryu Suzuki*

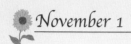

The heron's a saint when there are no fish in sight.

—*Bengalese Proverb*

One day, the Mullah Nasreddin was walking through a cemetery when he fell into an old grave. "How would it feel to be really dead?" he wondered. In this frame of mind he heard a noise, and it occurred to him that it must be the Angel of Reckoning coming to take him. In truth, it was only a caravan passing nearby.

Nasreddin leaped out of the grave and, stumbling, spooked the entire train of camels. It took the camel drivers a great while to recapture their beasts and, frustrated, they beat Nasreddin for having caused such a problem.

By the time he got home, Nasreddin was in quite a state. His wife asked him why he looked the way he did and why he was late.

"I have been dead," Nasreddin said matter-of-factly.

She could not resist. "Well then," she asked, "what is it like?"

"Oh, it's all right," Nasreddin answered, "as long as you don't upset the camels."

—*Traditional Sufi Story*

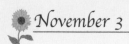

If you are reluctant to ask the way, you will be lost.
—*Malay Proverb*

This is the greatest success I can dream of for my life:
to have spread a new vision of the world.

—*Pierre Teilhard de Chardin*

It is said that a wise man rules over the stars,
but this does not mean that he rules over the influences
which come from the stars in the sky. It means that he rules
over the powers which exist in his own constitution.

—*Paracelsus*

There was a young man who had gone to school to learn things of the spirit. He considered himself to be a great teacher, but when he moved to a new town nobody came to listen to him.

Everybody there was already studying with a wise and well-respected rabbi. The young teacher was frustrated, so he figured out a way to make the rabbi look stupid. After that, he thought, people would come to him instead of to the master.

One day the young teacher caught a small bird and went to see the rabbi and his students. He strode right up to the rabbi, held out his hand, and said, "If you are so wise, tell us, is the bird in my hand alive or dead?"

If the rabbi said the bird was dead, the young man would open his hand, the bird would fly away, and the master would be shown to be foolish. If the rabbi said the bird was alive, the young man would swiftly crush the bird to death in his hand. Then he'd open it and say, "Look, the bird is dead." Either way the rabbi would be proven wrong and all the students would choose to study with the new teacher.

The young man was impatient. He demanded the rabbi answer. "Tell me now," he said, "if the bird is alive or dead!"

The rabbi looked at the young man and smiled. "My friend," he said, "the answer is entirely in your hands."

—Traditional Jewish Story

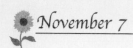

One hour of justice is worth a hundred of prayer.
—*Muslim Proverb*

Man is a ladder placed on the earth and the
top of it touches heaven. And all his movements and
doings and words leave traces in the upper world.

—*Traditional Chassidic Jewish Saying*

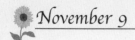

Those who bring sunshine to the faces of
others cannot keep it from themselves.

—*James M. Barrie*

Just as a few dead flies cause perfume to stink,
so do a few stupid acts ruin a reputation for wisdom.

—from the Book of Ecclesiastes
(Hebrew Scriptures)

It is the wind and the rain, O God, the cold and the storm
that make this earth of Thine to blossom and bear its fruit.
So in our lives it is storm and stress and hurt and suffering that
make real men and women bring the world's work to its
highest perfection.

—W. E. B. DuBois

Although the world is full of suffering,
it is also full of the overcoming of it.

—Helen Keller

A thankful person is thankful under all circumstances.
A complaining soul complains even if he lives in paradise.

—*Bahá'u'lláh*

Death was walking toward a city one morning and a man asked, "What are you going to do there?" "I'm going to take one hundred people," Death replied. "That's horrible!" the man said. "That's the way it is," Death said. "Well, we'll see about that," said the man as he hurried to warn everyone he could about Death's plan. As evening fell, he met Death again. "You told me you were going to take one hundred people," the man said. "Why did one thousand die?" "I kept my word," Death answered. "I only took one hundred. Worry took the rest."

—_Contemporary Spiritual Story_

In the hand that made the rose, shall I with trembling fall?
—*George Meredith*

If, in order to succeed in an enterprise,
I were obliged to choose between fifty deer commanded
by a lion, and fifty lions commanded by a deer,
I should consider myself more certain of success
with the first group than with the second.

—*St. Vincent de Paul*

In terms of space, the universe embraces
me and swallows me up like an atom;
still by my thought I may embrace the universe.

—Pascal

A man in charge of sacrifices to the gods gave his assistants a single goblet of wine. One apprentice said to the others, "There isn't enough here for all of us to drink. Let's each draw a snake in the dirt, and the one who finishes first can drink the wine." They agreed and began drawing. The first to finish his snake reached for the goblet and was about to drink. But as he held the wine in his left hand, he still kept drawing with the other. "I can draw feet for it," he said. But before he was done, another man finished drawing and grabbed the goblet from him, saying, "No snake has feet." And he drank up the wine.

—*Kuo Hsiang*

Right is right, even if everyone is against it;
and wrong is wrong, even if everyone is for it.

—*William Penn*

God gives nothing to those who keep their arms crossed.
—*West African Proverb*

The worst sin toward our fellow creatures
is not to hate them, but to be indifferent to them.

—*George Bernard Shaw*

But what is it that I love when I love You? Not the beauty of any bodily thing, nor the order of seasons; not the brightness of light that rejoices the eye, nor the sweet melodies of all songs; not the sweet fragrance of flowers and ointments and spices, nor manna or honey, nor the limbs that carnal love embraces. None of these things do I love in loving my God.

Yet when that light shines upon my soul which no place can contain, that voice sounds which no tongue can remove, I breathe that fragrance which no wind scatters, I eat the food which is not lessened by eating, and I lie in the embrace which satisfaction may never be taken from me. That is what I love, when I love my God.

—*St. Augustine of Hippo*

We expect too much of God,
but He always seems ready.

—*John F. Kennedy*

Heracles was journeying on a narrow road when he saw what looked like an apple on the ground. When he stepped on it, the object instantly became twice as big. Seeing the extraordinary growth, Heracles stepped on it with both feet and smashed it mightily with his club. As a result, the thing expanded so rapidly it blocked the road. Heracles threw down his club and stared at it dumbfounded.

The goddess Athena appeared to him then and said, "Dear brother, leave that thing alone! It is the spirit of argument and disharmony. If you keep from touching it, it can do no harm. But, as you have seen, if you try to fight, it only grows greater."

—Fable of Aesop

What is man without the beasts?
If all the beasts were gone, men would die from a great
loneliness of spirit. For whatever happens to the beasts,
soon happens to man. All things are connected.

—*Chief Seattle*

We never know how high we are till we are called to rise.

—*Emily Dickinson*

First a person should put his house together,
then his town, then the world.

—*Rabbi Israel Salanter*

When King David was still a boy watching over his father's sheep, he often came upon spiders' webs strung across tree branches and shining in the sun. David thought the spiders were wonderful to weave such webs, but he could see no use for them.

David decided to ask God about it. "Why, O Creator of the world, did you make spiders? You can't even wear their webs as clothing!" God answered David, "A day will come when you will need the work of this creature. Then you will thank me."

David grew up and became a courageous warrior. He defeated the giant Goliath and many enemies of the people of Israel. He married King Saul's daughter and the people adored him as the greatest man in the land.

Nonetheless, King Saul was jealous and afraid of David and sent his soldiers to kill him. David ran away to the wilderness in hopes that King Saul's anger would pass and he could return. But King Saul's men kept chasing him.

At last, the soldiers were very close. David ran into a cave to hide. He heard the footsteps of the men and knew that they would soon find him. David was so afraid his bones shook and hurt.

But then he saw a big spider at the front of the cave. Very quickly, it was spinning a web all the way across the opening.

Just before the soldiers came up to the cave, the spider finished its work. As the men started to enter, they ran into the web. "Look," they said, "this web is unbroken. If David were here, he'd have torn it to pieces. He must be hiding somewhere else. Let's go!"

So because of the spider, David's life was saved. David understood that God was wise and thanked God for creating all the creatures, including the spiders.

—Traditional Jewish Story

No duty is more urgent than that of returning thanks.
—*St. Ambrose*

No one can make you feel inferior without your consent.
—*Eleanor Roosevelt*

Whoever is small, is big. But whoever is big, is small.
—*from the Zohar*
(Ancient Mystical Text of Judaism)

Rabbi Akiva traveled with a donkey to lighten his load, a rooster to awaken him at dawn, and an oil lamp to study by at night. He trusted in God and believed that all God does is for the good.

One day, God made it that Rabbi Akiva arrived at a town after the gates had been closed, so he had to sleep outside in the dangerous woods. When he, at last, sat down to study by the light of his lamp, a great wind arose and blew it out. So, saying to himself "All is for the good," he lay down to sleep, confident the rooster would wake him early the next morning.

But then a fox came and carried the rooster away. Rabbi Akiva said, "This too will be for the good," and with that fell asleep. In the middle of the night, a lion pounced on the donkey and devoured the animal before it made a sound. Rabbi Akiva mourned over the life of his donkey, but saying "Everything is surely for the good," he found joy and comfort and returned to a deep sleep.

When Rabbi Akiva awoke in the morning, he saw that the town had been attacked and burned to the ground. "See," he said, "all is truly for the good. If I had gained entry into the town, or if my lamp had remained bright, or if my rooster had crowed, or my donkey brayed, these attackers who destroyed the town would have certainly come after me, too!"

—*Traditional Jewish Story*

Ambrosia can be extracted even from poison;
elegant speech even from a child;
good conduct even from an enemy;
gold even from impurity.

> —*from the Laws of Manu*
> *(Sacred Text of Hinduism)*

Always do right.
This will gratify some people,
and astonish the rest.

—*Mark Twain*

How far that little candle throws his beams.
So shines a good deed in a naughty world.

—*William Shakespeare*

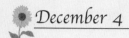

Do not neglect to show hospitality to strangers,
for thereby some have entertained angels unaware.

—*from Paul's Letter to the Hebrews*
(New Testament)

A visitor came to see a sick man and asked what ailed him. After the sick man told him, the visitor said: "Oh, my father died of that same disease." The sick man became terribly anxious, but the visitor said, "Don't worry, I'll pray to God to heal you." To which the sick man answered: "And when you pray, add that I may be spared visits from stupid people like you."

—*Traditional Jewish Story*

You have been granted, with your birth on this planet earth, extensive privileges. The establishment strongly requests you follow this guide:

1. You may go anywhere you wish (as long as you pay the bills).
2. You must check in regularly.
3. Your visa may be revoked at any time with or without notice.
4. Most services are provided freely (ask management about details).
5. Enjoy your stay.

—*Aaron Zerah*

A soldier approached the monk Hakuin and demanded of him, "Tell me, is there really such a thing as heaven and hell?"

"Who are you?" Hakuin asked.

The soldier answered, "I am a samurai warrior."

"Ha!" Hakuin laughed at him. "You, a samurai! What kind of lord would take in a fellow like you? You look like nothing more than a common beggar in the streets."

The soldier became furious and began to draw his sword, but Hakuin kept on: "So you have a sword, do you? I'll bet it's so dull you couldn't cut my head off with it, even if you wanted to!"

With that, the enraged soldier lifted his sword above the monk's head, and Hakuin said, "Now the gates of hell are opening."

The soldier, hearing these words, put back his sword and bowed in reverence to the monk.

"And," said Hakuin, "now open the gates of heaven."

—*Traditional Zen Buddhist Story*

An anxious heart weighs a man down,
but a kind word cheers him up.

> —*from the Book of Proverbs*
> *(Hebrew Scriptures)*

He who forces time is forced back by time,
but he who yields to time finds time standing at his side.

—*from the Babylonian Talmud*
(Sacred Book of Judaism)

It is the wisest who grieve most at the loss of time.

—*Dante*

Do not walk through time without leaving
worthy evidence of your passage.

—*Pope John XXIII*

It is time to come to your senses. You are to live
and to learn to laugh. You are to learn to listen to
the cursed radio music of life and to reverence the
spirit behind it and to laugh at its distortions. So
there you are. More will not be asked of you.

—*Herman Hesse*

Eighty percent of success is just showing up.
—*Woody Allen*

Success consists of getting up
just one more time than you fall.
—*Oliver Goldsmith*

Do not store up for yourselves treasures on earth,
where moth and rust destroy,
and where thieves break in and steal.
But store up for yourselves treasures in heaven,
where moth and rust do not destroy,
and where thieves do not break in and steal.
For where your treasure is,
there your heart will be also.

—*Jesus*

What is life? It is a flash of a firefly in the
night. It is a breath of a buffalo in the wintertime.
It is as the little shadow that runs across the
grass and loses itself in the sunset.

—*Chief Isapwo Muksika Crowfoot*

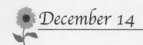

Think of all the beauty still left
around you and be happy.

—Anne Frank

The Earth is beautiful
The Earth is beautiful
The Earth is beautiful
The top of its head is beautiful
Its legs, they are beautiful
Its body, it is beautiful
Its chest, it is beautiful
Its breath, it is beautiful
Its head-feather, it is beautiful
The Earth is beautiful.

—Traditional Dineh/Navajo
Tribal Song (Native American)

God is beautiful and loves beauty.

—Traditional Muslim Saying

Where the spirit does not work with
the hand, there is no art.

—*Leonardo da Vinci*

One day, while hunting, two brothers stumbled on a magic fish hidden in a tree. The older brother was cautious, but the younger brother had a great hunger in his belly. He grasped the fish and ran home with it in great haste. There he immediately cooked and greedily devoured the magic fish.

By the next day, the young man had himself become a fish. Soon other people came to fish from the magic pond, but the voracious hunter-turned-fish would have none of that. He turned into a great bear and killed a member of each fishing party. A council was called and decided that if the bear lived, the people would be destroyed. Three men were chosen to kill the bear, but they failed and never returned. Finally, the older brother went to kill what his brother had become. He could not do so, but because he pursued the bear so doggedly, the bear, exhausted, agreed to leave his homeland. Once the bear had gone, the fish were plentiful again and the people prospered.

—*Traditional Seneca Tribal Tale*
(Native American)

An honest answer is like a kiss on the lips.
—*from the Book of Proverbs*
(Hebrew Scriptures)

Soyen Shaku, the abbot, each morning took a walk to the nearby town, accompanied by his assistant from the monastery. One day, as the abbot passed a house, he heard a great cry from within. Stopping to inquire, he asked the inhabitants, "Why are you all wailing so?" They said, "Our child has died and we are grieving." Without hesitation, the abbot sat down with the family and started crying and wailing himself. As they were returning to the monastery, the abbot's companion asked, "Master, is this family known to you?" "No," the abbot answered. "Why then, Master, did you also cry?" The abbot said simply, "So that I may share their sorrow."

—*Traditional Zen Buddhist Story*

We would often be sorry if our wishes were fulfilled.

—from a Fable of Aesop

The world will never starve for want of wonders,
but only for want of wonder.

—G. K. Chesterton

From the Unreal lead me to the Real.
From Darkness lead me to Light.
From Death lead me to Immortality.

> —*from the Upanishads*
> *(Sacred Text of Hinduism)*

No snowflake falls in an inappropriate place.
     —*Traditional Zen Buddhist Saying*

When you make peace with yourself,
you make peace with the world.

—*Maha Ghosananda*

The prophets are one family of God. Some have come in one country, some in another. But they belong to us all. If we celebrate the day of our prophet and criticize others, it is my feeling that our prophet will not be pleased, and we will never become enlightened. God has emphasized the same message through each prophet: "Go and teach the people love, teach them how to live well, take away their fears and their evils." In essence, all prophets sacrificed to create good human beings.

—*Baba Virsa Singh*

You are the light of the world.

—*Jesus*

What you have may seem small; you desire so much more.
See children thrusting their hands into a narrow-necked jar,
striving to pull out the sweets. If they fill the hand,
they cannot pull it out and then they fall to tears.
When they let go of a few, then they can draw out the rest.

—*Epictetus*

I matter to God as He does to me.
—*Angelus Silesius*

When you get to the end of your rope,
tie a knot and hang on. And swing!

—Leo Buscaglia

I have been to the end of the earth. I have been
to the end of the waters. I have been to the end of
the sky. I have been to the end of the mountains.
I have found none that were not my friends.

> —*Traditional Native*
> *American Prayer Song*

The Baal Shem Tov, may he be remembered, used to go to a certain place in the forest whenever he faced an especially difficult situation. There he would light a fire and pray, and whatever needed to be done was done.

After the Baal Shem Tov died, his successor followed in his footsteps, and he, too, went to the very same place in the forest. He said, "We cannot light the fire anymore, for we don't know the Master's way with it, but we can say the prayer." And whatever he asked in prayer was, as before, done.

This generation passed, and the new rabbi went to the woods and said, "The fire we are unable to light, and the prayer is gone from our minds. All we know is this holy place in the forest, and that will have to do." His prayers also came to be.

In the fourth generation, the rabbi no longer made the journey to the holy place. He stayed at home, for, as he said, "The fire we cannot light, the prayer we don't know anymore, nor do we remember the right place to go. All we can do is tell the story."

And that, too, was quite enough.

—*Traditional Chassidic Jewish Story*

It is at the year's end that
the fisherman tells of his fishing.

—*Gaelic Proverb*

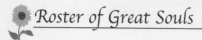

Roster of Great Souls

Aesop (c. 6th century BCE): Ancient Greek storyteller

Aha of Shabha (680-752): Babylonian scholar and writer

Ali (c. 602-661): Arabian; Muhammad's son-in-law and disputed caliph of Islam

Muhammad Ali (Contemporary): African-American world boxing champion and convert to Islam

Woody Allen (Contemporary): American comedian, filmmaker, and writer

St. Ambrose (c. 339-397): Roman Catholic Bishop

Amenemope (c. 11th century BCE): Ancient Egyptian author whose *Instructions* read like the biblical Book of Proverbs

Hans Christian Andersen (1805-1875): Danish storyteller and writer

Eberhard Arnold (1883-1935): German founder of Society of Brothers

Attar (died c. 1229): Persian Sufi mystic and poet

St. Augustine of Hippo (354-430): North African convert to Christianity and author of the autobiographical *Confessions*

Bahá'u'lláh (1817-1892): Persian prophet and founder of the Baha'i faith

Pearl Bailey (1918-1990): African-American singer, entertainer, and Goodwill Ambassador to the United Nations

Chilam Balam (c. 12th century): Mayan prophet known as the Jaguar Priest

James M. Barrie (1860-1937): Scottish playwright and author of *Peter Pan*

Karl Barth (1886-1968): Swiss theologian and professor who defied Hitler's edicts

St. Benedict (c. 480-547): Post-Roman founder of Christian monastic tradition

St. Bernard of Clairvaux (1090-1153): French Catholic monk and mystical writer

William Blake (1757-1827): English poet, painter, and mystic

Martin Buber (1878-1965): Austrian-born Jewish philosopher and author of *I and Thou*

Buddha (c. 563 BCE-c. 483 BCE): Indian prince who awakened to spiritual realization

Robert Burns (1759-1796): Scotland's most renowned poet

Leo Buscaglia (1924-1998): American philosopher of hugs and love

John Cage (1912-1992): American composer of experimental new music

Joseph Campbell (1904-1987): American scholar who renewed interest in mythology

Albert Camus (1913-1960): French existentialist writer, WWII resistance fighter, and Nobel Prize winner

Thomas Carlyle (1795-1881): Scottish historian, philosopher, and social critic

Pablo Casals (1876-1973): World-famous Spanish cellist and composer

G. K. Chesterton (1874-1936): English Roman Catholic essayist and writer of detective stories

Muhammad Muinuddin Chishti (1142-1236): Indian who helped establish a Sufi order founded on music

Chuang-tzu (c. 370 BCE-c. 286 BCE): Chinese philosopher and a principal founder of Taoism

Leonard Cohen (Contemporary): Canadian poet and songwriter

Samuel Taylor Coleridge (1772-1834): English lyric poet

Colette (1873-1954): French authoress of sensual, naturalistic novels

Confucius (c. 552 BCE-c. 479 BCE): Chinese philosopher, sage, and teacher

Joseph Conrad (1857-1924): Polish-born English seaman-turned-writer of exotic stories and novels

Chief Crazy Horse (c. 1849-1877): Oglala/Sioux who defeated Custer and was later killed resisting capture

Dalai Lama (Contemporary): Tibetan-born; Tenzin Gyatso is the fourteenth Dalai Lama (Ocean of Wisdom) and winner of the Nobel Peace Prize

Dante (1265-1321): Italian Romantic poet and author of *The Divine Comedy*

Baba Hari Dass (Contemporary): Indian-born American guru; silent for over forty years

Leonardo da Vinci (1452-1519): Italian painter, scientist, and genius

Miles Davis (1926-1991): Celebrated African-American trumpeter and composer of "cool jazz"

Dorothy Day (1897-1980): American social activist and co-founder of the *Catholic Worker* newspaper

Simone de Beauvoir (1908-1986): French existentialist novelist whose book *The Second Sex* stimulated the feminist movement

Pierre Teilhard de Chardin (1881-1955): French Catholic priest and paleontologist who created a new philosophy of evolution

Agnes de Mille (1905-1993): American dancer and choreographer

St. Vincent de Paul (1580-1660): French priest who founded a women's society to help the poor

St. Francis de Sales (1567-1622): French Catholic co-creator of a new spiritual order

Emily Dickinson (1830-1886): Reclusive American poet

Walt Disney (1901-1966): American cartoonist who created Mickey Mouse and Disneyland

John Donne (1573-1631): English adventurer, poet, preacher, and metaphysician

W. E. B. DuBois (1868-1963): African-American professor and civil rights activist who at age ninety-one moved to Africa

Meister Eckhart (c. 1260-1327): German priest and mystic accused of heresy

Thomas Edison (1847-1931): American inventor of (among other things) the lightbulb, the phonograph, and movies

Albert Einstein (1879-1955): German-born Jewish physicist who revealed the Theory of Relativity

Duke Ellington (1899-1974): African-American jazz composer, pianist, and bandleader

Ralph Waldo Emerson (1803-1882): American minister and writer who developed the philosophy of transcendentalism

Epictetus (c. 55-c. 135): Roman slave who became a Stoic philosopher

Desiderius Erasmus (c. 1466-1536): Dutch humanist and writer

Abraham ibn Ezra (1092-1167): Spanish Jewish scholar and poet

Fa-Chao (c. 8th century): Chinese Buddhist poet

Fa-Yen (885-958): Chinese Zen Buddhist monk and teacher

St. Francis of Assisi (1181-1226): Italian monk who gave up wealth and a military career to help the poor and seek peace between Christians and Muslims

Anne Frank (1929-1945): Dutch Jewish girl who hid from the Nazis but eventually was captured and killed; her diary captivated the world

Viktor Frankl (1905-1997): Austrian Jewish Holocaust survivor and author of *Man's Search for Meaning*

Benjamin Franklin (1706-1790): American philosopher and author who helped write the Declaration of Independence

Robert Frost (1900-1980): One of America's most celebrated poets

Mohandas Gandhi (1869-1948): Indian spiritual leader (known as Mahatma, or Great Soul) who preached and practiced nonviolence

Chief Dan George (1899-1981): Tell-lall-wwatt Indian (Canada) spiritual leader, Oscar-nominated film actor, and environmental spokesperson

Maha Ghosananda (Contemporary): Cambodian Buddhist and global Interfaith spiritual leader

Kahlil Gibran (1883-1931): Syrian-born American mystic, poet, and painter

Johann Wolfgang von Goethe (1749-1832): German philosopher, scientist, and author of *Faust*

Oliver Goldsmith (1728-1774): Irish poet and playwright

Billy Graham (Contemporary): American Christian evangelist who has preached all over the world

George Gurdjieff (1877-1949): Georgian-born mystic and spiritual teacher

Rabbi Moshe Hakotun (Unknown): Legendary Jewish sage

Thich Nhat Hanh (Contemporary): Vietnamese-born Buddhist monk who teaches meditation as a path to peace

Rabbi Abraham Heschel (1907-1972): Polish-born American Jewish scholar, civil rights activist, and religious dialogist

Herman Hesse (1877-1962): German-born novelist and mystic whose books were banned by the Nazis

Rabbi Hillel (died early 1st century): Jewish sage who lived in Jerusalem and taught kindness, like his successor, Jesus

Gerard Manley Hopkins (1844-1889): English Jesuit priest and poet

Aldous Huxley (1894-1963): English novelist and early experimenter with hallucinogenic drugs

Henrik Ibsen (1828-1906): Norwegian playwright and early feminist

William James (1842-1910): American philosopher and psychologist

Jesus (c. 4 BCE-c. 30 CE): Jewish rabbi whom Christians revere as the Messiah, the Son of God

Pope John XXIII (1881-1963): Italian who initiated a great change in the Roman Catholic Church

St. John of the Cross (1542-1591): Spanish mystic, monk, and friend of St. Teresa of Avila

Samuel Johnson (1709-1784): English writer, lexicographer, and moralist

Erica Jong (Contemporary): American feminist novelist

Julian of Norwich (c. 1342-after 1413): English mystic and poet who saw God as mother and father

Kabir (died 1518): Indian saint and poet who saw no difference between people of different religions

Helen Keller (1880-1968): American writer who overcame both deafness and blindness

John F. Kennedy (1917-1963): American President—the youngest
in history and the first Roman Catholic

Hazrat Inayat Khan (1882-1927): Indian-born musician who
brought Sufism to the West and created the world's first Interfaith
worship service

Sören Kierkegaard (1813-1855): Danish theologian known as the
father of existentialism

Martin Luther King Jr. (1929-1968): African-American civil rights
activist whose dream of equality inspired millions; preached and
practiced nonviolence and won the Nobel Peace Prize

Ray Kroc (1902-1984): American entrepreneur and founder of
McDonald's

Elisabeth Kübler-Ross (Contemporary): Swiss-born American
author of *On Death and Dying*

Kuo Hsiang (died c. 312): Chinese Taoist scholar

Lao-tzu (Unknown): Legendary Chinese "Old Master" known as
the author of the Tao Te Ching and the founder of Taoism

Brother Lawrence (1605-1691): French foot soldier who became a
monk and discovered the grace of a simple life

Ursula K. Le Guin (Contemporary): American science fiction writer

Abraham Lincoln (1809-1865): American President during the
Civil War who eventually decreed the end of slavery

Jack London (1876-1916): American adventurer and novelist

Martin Luther (1483-1546): German Catholic priest whose "protest" sparked the Reformation and the birth of Protestant churches

Lu-Yu (732-804): Chinese poet and author of *The Book of Tea*

Moses Maimonides (1135-1204): Born a Jew in Muslim Spain, he wrote great philosophical and religious works, such as *Guide of the Perplexed*, in Arabic

Somerset Maugham (1874-1965): English doctor-turned-novelist

Mechtild of Magdeburg (1212-1297): German mystic and writer

Mencius (c. 391 BCE-c. 308 BCE): Early Confucianist philosopher of personal and social responsibility

George Meredith (1828-1909): English poet and novelist

Thomas Merton (1915-1968): French-born American mystic and convert to Catholicism who studied and taught Eastern spiritual practices

Michelangelo (1475-1564): Florentine master painter, sculptor, architect, and poet

Milarepa (1043-1123): Revered Tibetan Buddhist teacher who, according to legend, gave up his ideas of revenge and became a yogi

Henry Miller (1891-1980): American author of novels banned for their sexuality

Thomas More (1478-1535): English statesman and Roman Catholic martyr and saint

Muhammad (570-632): Mecca-born leader who received the Qur'an and became the Prophet of Islam

John Muir (1838-1914): Scottish-born American naturalist and one of the world's first environmentalists

Rabbi Nachman of Bratzlav (1771-1811): Polish Chassidic Jewish mystic and storyteller

Guru Nanak (1469-1539): First Sikh guru and founder of the Sikh religion; an accountant who received God's call and began a new life of teaching and preaching

Shah Naqshband (1317-1389): Central Asian Sufi master whose order has spread throughout the world

Pablo Neruda (1904-1973): Chilean poet and Nobel Prize winner

Isaac Newton (1642-1727): English scientist, theologian, and discoverer of the laws of gravity

Reinhold Niebuhr (1892-1971): American theologian who greatly influenced Christians to look at social and political issues

Florence Nightingale (1820-1910): English nurse called to God's service and renowned for her bravery in war

Anaïs Nin (1903-1977): French-born American avant-garde novelist best known for her published diaries

Origen (c. 185-c. 254): Egyptian Christian theologian who was one of the leading biblical scholars of the early Church

Paracelsus (1493-1541): Swiss alchemist, physician, and Kabbalist

Blaise Pascal (1623-1662): French mathematician and philosopher

William Penn (1644-1718): English-born Quaker and founder of what later became the State of Pennsylvania

Judaeus Philo (c. 25 BCE–c. 50 CE): Egyptian-born Jewish philosopher who became well-known throughout the Roman Empire

Pablo Picasso (1881–1973): Spanish painter and sculptor; still the world's most famous "modern" artist

Plato (c. 427 BCE–c 347 BCE): Greek philosopher and author of *The Republic*

Ptah-hotep (c. 2650 BCE): Ancient Egyptian; world's first writer to be known by name

Ramakrishna (1836–1886): Bengali mystic who taught that all religions are a path to the same goal

Vanessa Redgrave (Contemporary): English actor, Oscar winner, and political activist

Rainer Maria Rilke (1875–1926): German lyric poet and mystic

Tom Robbins (Contemporary): American novelist

Will Rogers (1879–1935): American humorist and actor known as the "cowboy philosopher"

Eleanor Roosevelt (1884–1962): Popular American First Lady, representative to the United Nations, and advocate of human rights

Franklin D. Roosevelt (1882–1945): American President who led the country during depression and war

Jellaludin Rumi (1207–1275): Anatolian Sufi mystic poet of divine love and creator of the "whirling dervish" ecstatic dances

Ryokan (1758–1831): Japanese Zen Buddhist monk and poet

Antoine de Saint Exupéry (1900-1944): French aviator and author of *The Little Prince*

Rabbi Israel Salanter (1810-1883): Lithuanian Jew who founded the highly ethical Musar movement

George Santayana (1863-1952): Spanish-born American philosopher and author

Rabbi Menachem Mendel Schneerson (1902-1994): Ukrainian-born American spiritual leader of the Lubavitcher Chassidic Jewish community

Chief Seattle (c. 1786-1866): Native American who reluctantly negotiated land treaties with the American government

Seneca (c. 4 BCE-65 CE): Roman dramatist and philosopher of the Stoic school

William Shakespeare (1564-1616): English poet and writer of the world's most well-known plays

George Bernard Shaw (1856-1950): Irish dramatist, writer, and social critic

Angelus Silesius (1624-1677): German priest and poet

Isaac Bashevis Singer (1904-1991): Polish-born Jewish-American writer and Nobel Prize winner

Baba Virsa Singh (Contemporary): Indian Sikh guru who leads an Interfaith community where all prophets are honored and all holidays observed

Chief Sitting Bull (1834-1890): Lakota/Sioux spiritual leader and medicine man who helped defeat Custer but years later was arrested and killed

Robert Louis Stevenson (1850-1894): Scottish novelist most famous for creating Dr. Jekyll and Mr. Hyde

Shunryu Suzuki (1905-1971): Japanese Zen master who founded one of America's first Zen centers, in San Francisco

Jonathan Swift (1667-1745): Anglo-Irish poet, satirist, and author of *Gulliver's Travels*

Rabindranath Tagore (1861-1941): Indian poet and philosopher; first Asian to win the Nobel Prize for Literature

Chief Tecumseh (1768-1813): Chief of the Shawnee who promoted peace among all tribes

Alfred, Lord Tennyson (1809-1892): English lyric poet

Mother Teresa (1910-1997): Albanian-born nun who served the "poorest of the poor" in India and for her work won the Nobel Peace Prize

St. Teresa of Avila (1515-1582): Spanish nun, mystic, and author of *The Interior Castle*

St. Thérèse of Lisieux (1873-1897): French nun whose autobiography is called, simply, *The Story of a Soul*

Henry David Thoreau (1817-1862): American philosopher and author of *Walden*

Howard Thurman (1900-1981): African-American minister and

civil rights leader who in San Francisco founded America's first truly Interfaith congregation

Sojourner Truth (1797-1883): American-born slave who became a leading abolitionist and women's rights advocate

Mark Twain (1835-1910): American humorist and creator of Tom Sawyer and Huckleberry Finn

Voltaire (1694-1778): French writer and philosopher; leading figure of the Enlightenment and catalyst of the French Revolution

George Washington (1732-1799): American Revolutionary War leader and first President of the United States

John Watson (1850-1907): Scottish clergyman and writer

Alan Watts (1915-1973): English-born American spiritual teacher of Eastern philosophies

H. G. Wells (1866-1946): English novelist, social progressive, and historian

John Wesley (1703-1791): English Christian evangelist and founder of Methodism

Walt Whitman (1819-1892): American poet most noted for his *Leaves of Grass*

Elie Wiesel (Contemporary): Hungarian-Jewish Holocaust survivor and Nobel Prize-winning author

Oscar Wilde (1854-1900): Irish dramatist and renowned wit

Marianne Williamson (Contemporary): American spiritual teacher and author

William Wordsworth (1770-1850): English lyric poet

Wilbur Wright (1867-1912): American who with his brother, Orville, built and flew the first airplane

Wu-Men (1183-1260): Chinese Zen Buddhist who literally stayed awake until he reached enlightenment

William Butler Yeats (1865-1939): Irish poet and Nobel Prize winner

Chief Yellow Lark (1854?-?): Sioux spiritual leader who shared the prayers of his people with non-natives

Paramahansa Yogananda (1893-1952): Indian-born yogi; one of the first to teach meditation in America

Aaron Zerah (Contemporary): Interfaith minister, teacher, and author

About the Author

Aaron Zerah is an Interfaith minister who embraces all people of spirit. He works with the Spirit of Interfaith and other global organizations to build a world of peace, and lives happily in beautiful British Columbia, Canada, with his four-year-old daughter, Sari.

KG